Horse Stories

The Healing Way Horses Teach Us Healthy Relationships

Gina E. Deleo Martell and Debra Johnson

Horse Stories

The Healing Way Horses Teach Us Healthy Relationships

Revision 1.0a

March, 2021

Published by: Remington Publications

1146 N. Central Ave., Suite 136

Glendale, CA 91202

323.638.4145

Cover Designer: Jeremy Wyngaard (jaywyngaard@yahoo.com)

Photos: Justin Wasilkowski - Photographer

George Butch – Photo Editor

ISBN: 978-0-9972462-6-1

Printed in the United States

The information in this book is opinion only and does not represent legal, medical or psychological advice. You should consult with a licensed practitioner for any professional advice.

Debra and I would like to thank Dennis Neder and Remington Publications for publishing our book. We are so honored that our first-time publishing experience has been not only a learning experience (and Dennis knows what we mean ... lol) but a true testament to how far someone will go to guide you and support you when they believe in you. Thank you, Dennis, for your insight, your time and your friendship! You made our dream come true!

Dedications

This book is lovingly dedicated to the horses that saved our lives:

Dodger, Blue, Tango, Eeyore, Jeffrey, Punk, Black Beauty, Regal Lady.

If it were not for you, we would not be who we are today.

Thank you for your magic!

Table of Contents

Table of Contents v

Debra's Introduction 7

Gina's Introduction 10

If We Could Talk to the Animals...Wait a Minute—We Can! 16

My Winter Vision 26

So, What was My Bottom? 31

Respect the Ride 43

From the Heart of Horses—Listen and You'll Learn 48

He Knew I was coming, so He Waited—Dodger's Story 58

Dodger's Journey Back to Himself 68

You've Got to Have Friends 78

Angels and Horses and Bad Apples.............................. 85

Coaching with Children: Katie and Clarice 91

Fear 99

Authenticity is All Important....................................... 111

Against the Wall.. 115

Teaghlach: Celtic for Family 122

Tug of War... 133

The Deepest Wounds Need the Deepest Healings 140

Addictions and the Horse.. 149

Dan Tangled Up in Blue.. 159

Standing in the Peace of a Horse 164

Debra's Thank You 170

Gina's Thank You 173

About the Authors 177

Index 182

Debra's Introduction

I wrote this book because I want to share the miracles I experienced with horses and my spiritual reawakening because of horses. Growing up, I spent many happy summers working on my grandparent's farm. It was a wondrous time for me as a little girl and I loved working with the animals and helping my grandparents with the daily chores of farm life. I loved tagging along with my grandfather and listening to his stories. I didn't mind being the willing participant of his practical jokes either.

My grandfather was from a different generation; he was born in 1896. I would listen to his stories of hauling horses from Wisconsin to Iowa in the late 1930's to the 1950's. Wisconsin agriculture was transitioning from horses to tractors and my grandfather bought horses from Wisconsin farmers and sold them to Iowa farmers, who for the most part, still used horses in agriculture.

I was eager to learn everything he knew about horses and asked him endless questions. My grandfather was always patient with me and answered each question with kindness and twinkle in his eye. One of my favorite memories was his answer to the question, "Grandpa, how do you ride horses?" "Get on and don't fall off." was his reply. Practical and to the point!

His wisdom was honest and simple. He told me many times, "If you can handle a pony, you can handle any horse you come across. Ponies may be small, but they're smart." Over the years, that statement has been proven true many times.

Those summers with my grandparents were golden. I learned so much about life and about horses. I am forever grateful for those days and times. As I grew up, I discovered the Martial Arts, studied art in college, owned my own Martial Arts business, became a substitute teacher and worked as an Equine Specialist at a nonprofit mental health facility.

Sometimes my life seemed like a giant jigsaw puzzle with unrelated life experiences laid out in front of me. It was only when I began to work as an Equine Specialist that I saw the pieces fit together. The chi, or energy studies from the Martial Arts training helped me sense the energy that surrounds all things, especially horses.

The creativity in art, helped find innovative ways of working with horses. Working as a substitute teacher helped me translate what the horse was communicating to clients. The most important thing I have learned so far from horses has been, when I entered the horse world on their terms, magic and miracles have followed.

Gina's Introduction

This book was written to honor those who bravely and courageously come to work with me to improve their lives, those who are also asked to believe that a horse is going to help them! That takes faith in the horse, in me, and in the process of equine-assisted life coaching.

It has also been written to help open the eyes and hearts of anyone that owns a horse and may be missing out on the beautiful, honest relationship that a horse can bring to their life.

Though the names have been changed, in telling the stories of some of my coaching clients, I hope to show others that they are not alone in the issues they are facing. So many of us have gone through sorrow and pain and have felt like giving up. I hope to show the magic of how effective it can be to not just work with a life coach, but also to share themselves with my horses.

I have loved horses my whole life. I have always known they were special. As I grew up, I would make deals with my parents and grandparents, proposing that they should "Just get me a horse and you never have to get me another gift ever!"

When my parents got divorced, I finally got my first horse at the age of ten. Her name was Black Beauty. It was 1970. I had no saddle, and I learned to ride bareback. After I finally got a saddle, I began going to horse shows every weekend in Miami and around Florida. I learned to barrel race and ride Western Pleasure style. I won a lot of ribbons and trophies. Beauty taught me a lot, and I read and studied and listened to every bit of information I could glean about horses.

My mother moved us around a lot. I would always find friends with horses that had problems. I could always fix the horses' behavior, but what I came to realize in my teens was that no matter how well I fixed someone's horse, it was the human that was the actual problem. Ostensibly, my experience with horses comes from having and training horses since I was ten, but through the years, my best teachers and what gave me the most knowledge about horses were my horses themselves!

I'd had a rough childhood with an alcoholic mom and abusive stepfather, so I'd spent a lot of time talking to and riding my horse. Horses in general were my most trusted friends, next to a few childhood friends that remain today. Sometimes I'd go sleep in the stall of my palomino dun Quarter Horse, Punk, when things in the house got scary.

I have always revered animals and nature and feel deeply connected on a spiritual level to them. I also have a strong intuitive sense, oftentimes called "the touch." It may have been passed on to me from my grandfather, Joseph Stafford Rhodes, whom neither my mother nor I knew. My grandfather was reportedly a horse trainer and handler in the circus and in rodeos from roughly 1940 to 1960. They said he had a special gift for handling horses, and maybe I inherited it from him. Either way, I am grateful for it.

In my almost sixty years, I have owned and loved six horses. The first four were there to protect me and keep me on a straight path during my somewhat treacherous youth.

In 2009, because of my natural intuition and desire to help others, I decided to pursue a career as a life coach. I volunteered for about five years with international motivational speaker and coach Tony Robbins on the Fire Team, learning how to build the fire lanes of hot coals that everyone who attends his seminars walks on. Fire walking is a metaphor for stepping into your fears and changing your life! I studied his techniques and took the International Coaching Federation (ICF) course from The Life Coaching Institute.

I just threw myself into everything that was about spiritual healing, growth, coaching work, and techniques. I studied online with my dear friend and mentor, Dr. Dennis Neder. He is also a chiropractor, has a degree in psychology, and is also a life coach. I read a lot of Wayne Dyer and Abraham Hicks, and then I began coaching firefighters, police officers, and couples. I didn't charge for my services because I considered it my internship.

Once I became certified as a life coach, I continued my studies with transformative coach, author, and hypnotist David Key in the U.K. and took his course on

Neurolinguistic Programing (NLP). By now I had been working with clients for almost eight years.

Roughly a year after that, I studied with master equine coach Pam Kachelmeier online and in Wisconsin to do an intensive, hands-on course with the horses. With Pam, it was all about being authentic and understanding deeply the energy of horse. My prior horse experience was nothing compared to what I learned from Pam and the horse.

Then it was about almost a year after that that I obtained my certification in Pam's course for equine-assisted coaching (EAC). After turning in a paper, providing almost twenty hours of notes, and working one-on-one with clients, I am now a member of Equine-Assisted Coaching Association (EACA).

But the studying and education never stops! I must stay on top of everything and anything that can help me become a better coach. There are many great teachers out there, and I learned to not be stuck to just one. I can and do learn from all of them, and I love it!

My current horses, Dodger and Blue, are here at this chapter of my life to guide me through my current journey—to not only teach me every day about their world, but also to partner together with me to help the once broken become whole again.

Meeting Debra Johnson, my co-writer, has been such a blessing. Debra and I met at Pam's class in Wisconsin, and we just instantly hit it off! I could sense she was empathic and had some truly spiritual gifts.

A year after meeting Debra, I was asked to present at a coaching seminar that Pam was hosting, and Debra attended it as well. Debra's energy and obvious spiritual abilities intrigued me, and I said to her, "You have spiritual things you can teach me. And you are going to, right?" Debra laughed and said she noticed the same thing about me. We realized we both had something special when we could both see the spirit of a little black cat at my feet and no one else could!

That is when we decided to stay in touch. One day after many conversations about our love of horses and coaching, she lightly said, "We should write a book," to which I said, "YES!"

It was a no brainer to co-write with Debra because our views on handling horses are so similar. I meet few people that have as much as passion as I do about horses—Debra definitely does.

We confer together over clients, we discuss cool things to do with the horses, and we get super excited at how magical this work is. We both wanted to share our mutual love and understanding for horses with the world.

In 1965, Gina at age five on her favorite pony from Dodge City Pony Rides in Miami, Florida.

If We Could Talk to the Animals...Wait a Minute—We Can!

"The Horse does one of two things. He does what he thinks he's supposed to do, or he does what he thinks he needs to do to survive."—Ray Hunt

I believe humans can talk to horses and that, many eons ago, man had the ability to understand the animal kingdom. Anna Breytenbach, one of my personal favorite animal communicators, discussed this subject in a seminar she gave in South Africa back in 2016. Anna became an interspecies communicator, animal activist, conservationist, and public speaker. She lives in Cape Town, South Africa, and her work in communicating with wild animals is impressive.

Her work with wild jaguars, baboons, and the rest of the wild kingdom in South Africa is a far leap from her previous career in IT with a degree in psychology. I have spoken with a few animal communicators about this gift we seem to all possess, this ability to communicate with other species, which includes plants and trees. Skeptics become believers when they watch a video of Anna calming down an angry jaguar by bringing herself through meditation to his level and then being able to interpret emotions and pictures, he is sending her.

She also was able to communicate with and explain to wild baboons in the area to stop attacking the garbage and jumping at people who were simply walking to their automobiles. She is routinely able to pick up from her animal client's information that verifies a truth that only that animal's handler would know. In short, Breytenbach is absolutely amazing! You can find out more about her on YouTube!

So, do "regular" humans have this ability to communicate with animals? I believe we do and, even in my own humble experience listening to my horses, I have to believe that Anna and many other interspecies communicators are not making this up. However, with our largely lost connection to nature, perhaps it's a power that's suppressed until we choose to become open in our hearts and minds.

So many of us alive today have replaced our innate connection to the earth with a reliance on technology and all the busy-ness and stress that comes with modern life. The result is we have lost our ability to connect not just with the animals but also with plants and trees as well. We have forgotten how to commune with nature.

Humans tend to see ourselves as more powerful and important than nature. Much as a rancher might see a wild horse on the open plain, we view Gaia[1] (Mother Nature) as something to be conquered and tamed. We suppress her beneath slabs of asphalt and blocks of cement and keep her contained behind tidy fences and gates. We forget that nature should be as wild and free as we once were ourselves. In forgetting who Mother Nature is and her importance to us, we have forgotten who we are. But luckily many of us are coming back to remembering.

This disconnect from our primal roots is a huge reason humanity is struggling. How has this disconnection from nature affected your life? Pause a moment and ask

---

[1] In Greek mythology, Gaia was the goddess of the Earth and ancestral mother of all life, also referred to as Mother Nature.

yourself these questions: When is the last time you slowed down and sat in the grass barefoot and listened to the birds chirping? Have you taken a moment today to take a deep breath of fresh air? Even if you live in the city, a walk in the park or a walk on the beach can do so much for you!

Are you able to take time from your busy schedule for a walk on a nature trail or just around the block and admire the flowers, both those growing wild or in manicured gardens? When you travel from place to place, do you take a moment to notice the blueness of the sky and the fluffiness of the clouds? Do you ever go outside at night just to look at the moon and stars? Even if you live in a city where unfettered nature seems scarce, a connection with Gaia is your birthright, a gift that provides happiness and healing in so many ways. It's important to seek ways to connect with her.

Have you taken a moment today to create that connection? Animals, on the other hand/hoof/paw, etc., don't need to consciously seek out a connection to their natural surroundings. Out of necessity, horses have a greater ability to perceive their environment than do humans. Equines are prey animals motivated by instinct, which makes them completely aware in the moment. And like any prey animal—from the wilds of Africa to the back alley where feral cats live—they are instinctively aware that they can be killed at any time, so they must be hypersensitive to their surroundings to survive.

Every fiber of a horse's physical body picks up and processes information from the environment. Their ears pick up the smallest distant sounds from several miles away. Their nostrils gather information from the faintest scent. Their eyes, which are located on the side of their heads, see panoramically, up to 350 degrees. Because their vision is mostly monocular, they used both eyes separately. The hairs on their bodies catch the lightest breeze. Touch and smell are also tools, as their whiskers let them know when something is too close or sharp or dangerous like an electric fence.

Horses are sentient beings with consciousness and emotions. Because of their natural instincts and connection to the earth, horses possess energy like all living beings. It is understanding and tapping into this energy that is so important when partnering with horses for equine coaching.

Furthermore, understanding horse communication within the herd can teach you a great deal about your horse and will help you in communicating with her better when riding her or simply loading her into a trailer.

For example, horses' body language and posture are big indicators that something is up. Horses can sense inclement weather coming and may lie down or stand together in their herd with their backs to the wind. Their communication with each other is full of nickering, snorting, squealing, and whinnies. Horses are social creatures and, living in a herd, communication and all those tiny micro movements like a flick of an ear or a raise of the head matter to their own and the herd's survival.

When a human enters a horse's field of vision, the horse instantly and intuitively knows everything it needs to know to decide how it's going to interact with that person. Horses don't care about *who* the human is; they care *what* the human is. They aren't fooled by fronts—fancy boots, fake smiles, and whatnot. They can read our emotional state and can sense the energies we project. If we are feeling nervous, angry, afraid, or happy, they can tell. They ask the question, "What will you do to me?"

Throughout history, horses have worked for humans. So, it seems perfectly natural for us to approach the horse with the question, "What will you do for me?" But instead of taking this approach, what if, when we meet a horse for the first time, we stopped thinking about what can the horse do for us, but rather what can we learn from the horse? Some questions to ask yourself before diving in to make the horse work for you include:

- Who is this horse? Where does it come from? How old is it? What is its gender?
- What is its history? Has the horse experienced abuse or abandonment? What were its jobs?
- What is its rank in the herd? A horse's rank depends on its age and personality.
- What is the horse sensing about me?

Also, instead of asking "What can this horse do for me?" ask the questions "What kind of a relationship can I create with my horse?" and "Who will my horse and I be together?"

These questions can help you build better relationships in the human world, too, as sometimes we need to pause and ask questions like this to better understand the humans with whom we are interacting.

Humans love words and our realities are mainly created and exist within the confines of language. We use words like *team*, *leader,* and *control* to define relational dynamics. However, words don't exist in the horse world, only energy does. To truly know your horse, there needs to be a shift in the paradigm of human thinking.

If humans can learn to communicate with their horse on the individual horse's terms through communicative energy, the relationship will be healthier and more productive. In other words, instead of trying to be the "leader" take a moment to feel the energy that comes from the word. Is that how you want to communicate with your horse? By overpowering him or do you want to partner with him? A good leader isn't the boss over the other. At heart, a good leader cares and is concerned for the other's best interest.

'Do you know your horse?", is not a question, but a challenge. The horse is a creation of the Divine. To know your horse, the modern way of thinking and interacting must stop. Stop thinking; start feeling. Not with words, but with energy.

Enter the horse's world the way we once did before the world sped up and we lost our way.

Enter your horse's field of vision not as a master, but as an equal.

By doing this you will reopen the healthy, natural lines of communication we once had many centuries ago with horses.

My Winter Vision

"Magic exists in the quiet moments, and miracles happen in the ordinary."—Debra Johnson

January in northeast Wisconsin can be a mixed bag of low temperatures and high snow drifts. This specific morning in 2012 wasn't one for the record books, but it was close. The thermostat was in the double-digits below zero and had been like that for a few days. It was the kind of cold that always makes me gasp for breath as I get out of my warm vehicle. With each step around the barn where I work, the ten inches of snow made a squeaking, crunching sound under my boots that raised in pitch as the temperature drops. And, naturally, the cold motivated me to move more quickly through my tasks.

I work at an equine-assisted mental health center in Shiocton, Wisconsin, and we rely on help from volunteers to run smoothly. I started out as a volunteer there, too, and knew the commitment it took to brave the early morning cold to care for the horses. The volunteers are all fascinating, good-hearted people from all walks of life, and I enjoy working with them.

Our dedicated weekend volunteer, Manda, was no exception. She was a bright, young nursing student with a calm and gentle demeanor who wanted to work with newborns. I was going to be meeting with her that morning to introduce her to the four new horses that had recently been donated to the program and to go over a few changes to the feeding routine.

Focused on my tasks, I was hurrying to be ready by the time she arrived. When she got to the barn, we met in the thoroughfare and walked a few feet to the new indoor arena where the horses were stabled. I grabbed the handle on the arena's sliding door, gave it a tug, and the door slid open with a slight screech.

The barn swallows that sheltered inside were startled by our interruption and swooped about the arena in sporadic flight patterns, protesting loudly for a few minutes before settling back onto their roosts with calm chirps. As Manda and I walked, she smiled and mentioned how beautiful their wings looked as they flew through the sunlight that shone in scattered beams through the dusty arena windows.

I was caught off guard for a second. Sure, I loved the birds, too, but she was seeing them like an artist would. I felt an uncomfortable pinch in the center of my chest. Then I felt a memory (yes, I felt a memory) from when I was in art school. I loved seeing the world around me through artistic eyes. I hadn't created any art for a while, but in that moment, I felt a longing to get back to that part of myself.

Then, just as quickly, I was snapped back into the present moment and the tasks at hand, but in the back of my mind, I asked myself why Manda had seen the simple beauty in that moment, but I hadn't. As we walked across the arena, she and I talked about the feeding routine as our breath spun into vapor and danced over our heads in the chilly arena air. When I asked her if she was ready to meet one of the new horses, Manda smiled and nodded yes. I walked ahead to the first stall, slid the cold metal latch back and opened the door. The tall, brown, bay gelding came out and walked toward her. The two spent a moment together, and I asked her if she wanted to meet the other horses.

 Again, she smiled and nodded. As I opened each stall and each horse walked out, I heard Manda speaking softly to them. I couldn't tell what she was saying, but her tone sounded soft and soothing. Each horse approached to Manda one at a time to touch her outstretched hands. Sunbeams shone through the windows, enveloping the five beings in a circle of light.

I was instantly struck with the magic, beauty, and majesty of this scene—four equine souls and one human soul communicating in harmony. Emotions rushed through me like an electric current, but I immediately felt compelled to turn away like I wasn't worthy of witnessing it. Then I felt a tug inside of me, inviting me to turn back and look. I slowly turned my eyes toward Manda and the horses, and my body followed.

I watched in amazement as they communicated as equal beings on a deep, soul level. It was as if time had slowed down. I was witnessing what I wanted to be able to do with horses. I felt awe, but I also felt jealousy. Why did Manda get that magical connection with them as a volunteer they had known for minutes when I was there all the time?

Then it hit me. I was meant to be a part of this magic, too, but I had to change some things about myself. I had to slow down and not be so focused on getting tasks done that I missed the small miracles of which the horses would allow me to be a part. And, like Manda and her ability to see the beauty of the birds' wings in the sunlight, I had to adjust my vision. Now, I no longer rush from task to task around the barn. I take the time to be present and commune with the horses and stay open to what they want to show me—yes, even in double-digits below zero temps. As a result, my relationship with the horses has grown deeper than I ever imagined possible.

I'm so thankful for that majestic moment that showed me that when we slow down, see the beauty in simple things, and treat horses as equals instead of things in our charge, we can experience magic.

So, What was My Bottom?

"The only thing I can control is me"—Gina Martell

When you grow up like I did, life becomes an inner battle to become who you were destined to become. I look back now at the people who affected my young life and, because I live in consciousness every day, I have made the choice to forgive them. I'm not saying it was easy, but forgiving is the easier path. It is the path of my understanding that the events in my life were all put in place to help me become who I am today. For that reason alone, I am thankful that I am a strong warrior woman, a mother, a wife, a life coach, a friend, a sister—and a best friend to my horses.

My journey was rough. I had been married and divorced twice and was a mother of three young children. I constantly fought low self-esteem, was devoid of self-love, had zero confidence, and was dealing with a nagging anger problem. I was pissed-off and frustrated in my life and it had been that way for almost all my life. I was controlling and short-tempered and just mad at the world and everyone in it.

It's easy to blame everyone else for our problems. I was a victim. I lived my story of woe and unhappiness and believed I would never be happy. At twenty-seven, I married for the first time. By thirty-one I was divorced, had twin babies and was beginning my first career as an on-air radio personality for a station in Miami, Florida. When I turned thirty-seven, I married again and had another child. I was convinced this time would be better, but it wasn't. What was wrong with me?

My children were the only things that really made me happy and grateful. Being a mom was the best decision I'd ever made. I wanted to be a good mom and raise happy kids. I took my motherhood skills very personal. My own mother had not been very loving or supportive, just sporadically, when it benefited her. At least that is how it felt to me.

I always told myself that when I had kids, I would work really hard to be a great mom. Today, I look back and wonder how we survived all the challenges. I remember my daughter telling me when she was five that we all have angels and, "Mommy, you have a lot." Those beautiful little words I guess are what got me through it all at least.

In 2005, at the age of fourteen, my oldest son became a drug addict. He was so young and I was so devastated. It hit every trigger in my own life about my childhood and my mother and stepfather being alcoholics.

I sent my son to a rehab facility in Loa, Utah. His counselors had emphatically warned me that if I didn't move from Miami, my son would return to connect with the same friends and same environment and could relapse. They suggested I move to another state or far away from where I was, and I did. I moved my daughter and little son to Atlanta, Georgia.

I had been offered a job on TV for the Jewelry Channel and I had lived in Atlanta in my twenties and always loved it. So, we made the move. I was sure my son would come back to live with me there to have the fresh start he needed. My son was given a week off from his program to come to visit, but instead he told me he would be returning to Miami to live with his father.

We stayed in Atlanta for only four months, and I decided to move back to my Florida house and try to put things together again. When I returned to Miami, I had to fly out with his twin sister to meet the rehab counselors in Utah and go through a parent exercise. It was supposed to help my son and give the therapist a chance to meet the parents and help us work through our own stuff.

My decision to really participate and be open and vulnerable with the process was great for my son. However, it backfired on me with my ex-husband. He stood up in our little campfire group session with my son, other boys and their parents, and the therapist and told them all that I was a terrible mother.

His intentional choice to hurt me and be so mean was more than I could bear. I left the circle and ran to my little tent and cried myself to sleep. I was thankful the therapist really jumped on him and recommended he seek out therapy himself.

The next morning, I had decided. I sat on a huge rock in the desert area of Loa. I watched the sun rise and closed my eyes and forgave my ex-husband. I also decided right then that I wasn't going to allow myself to feel this way anymore!

I let go of a lot of things that day on that rock in the Utah desert. I accepted that I had not been a perfect parent. I had made mistakes and I also forgave myself for them. My load was lighter, and my son was very loving to me that day.

When I returned home in Miami, I sought out a therapist for myself. She was more of a coach/therapist herself and I really liked her. I told her she had to fix me, and I began working with her two days a week.

She did a lot of re-parenting. She recommended numerous books. We talked and I cried...a lot. I had so much buried inside of me. I was a giant Samsonite warehouse of baggage, and I began to understand why I chose the people I did to be significant in my life. I had so much to learn, but the most important thing I realized was I finally learning to love myself!

It took me decades to learn that one simple thing. To love myself despite how anyone else treated me. I was in my forties, my son still had his drug issues, and I had no control over him or his addiction. It just killed me seeing him loathe himself so much and yet, I knew I had to let him figure it out. I prayed a lot. I put him in God's hands, and I felt angels around him all the time. At this point in my life, I was more religious than spiritual. I wasn't open to much else. I did things differently than I would do them today.

At one point, I was just so tired and scared I felt like giving up. It had to be my son's choice to change his life, and I had to finish working on me to be able to help him more. I had tried everything and had no more money to send him to another rehab. I blamed myself. I blamed his father. I blamed everyone for my son's choices. What I didn't realize was, no matter what mistakes my ex, and I may have made through the years, my son's choices were HIS choices.

I didn't figure that out until I turned fifty. I had attended my thirty-year high school reunion and met up with an old friend. Justin was one of the nicest guys in our class back in 1978. He was Polish and had red hair. We had lost touch after high school, but later when we reconnected, he told me he always had a thing for me and regretted not having asked me out.

We laugh about that now, twelve years later! We began dating after the reunion. I was forty-nine years old then. After a year of dating, Justin gave the greatest gift ever. On my fiftieth birthday, he took me to an Unleash the Power Within (UPW) event with Tony Robbins. That event was the most intense work I had ever done on myself.

For four days, I arose early and sat in a freezing cold auditorium and listened. I wrote notes in my UPW notebook. I ate snacks and drank coffee to stay warm and awake. I wasn't giving up. I played full out, as Tony recommends. I gave one hundred percent of my pain, my tears, and myself – everything I had – to thousands of people I had never met but who became like family after those four days. It was amazing.

So, in New Jersey, on a freezing-cold, snowy winter night, I walked on a path of 1,800-degree-Fahrenheit burning coals barefoot and changed my life. When I left, my eyes and heart were open. I walked on fire not once but *twice* because it felt so fantastic to succeed and push myself to do something scary. I stopped being the victim. I changed my story. For the first time, I really saw who I was and who I could be. I had a purpose, and I was just scratching its surface.

It was there and then that I decided to become a life coach. I also decided to be open to becoming spiritual. My belief in God was now stronger than any religion I had followed. I was awake and I had a giant thirst to learn about intuition, energy, and healing. My path to become a healer was laid out before me like golden steps. All the right people began showing up in my life, and things started happening. I changed. I let things go, I lived in the flow, and I continued forgiving.

I had a way to go, but I knew that I was finally on the right path—the path of least resistance. I began seeking education on becoming a life coach and got my first certification as CPC, a certified professional coach, and then was so excited about that that I took a course for Neurolinguistic programming (NLP) and became certified in that, too.

After a few years of working with mostly women and couples, I married that man that gave me those awesome gifts of UPW and my life's subsequent transformation. Justin gave me the opportunity to change my life, and I will be forever thankful to him for that.

It wasn't long after we got married that we moved to Woodstock, Georgia, and bought a house on four acres. I adopted my two rescue horses, and those two horses are the reasons I am now an EACA—equine-assisted life coach.

One day, I went into the horse tack and feed store I frequent and saw the manager was having a bad day. I took a few minutes to talk to her and gave her my card. She got super excited and said, "You have to become an equine-assisted life coach."

I had to search the Internet for the course and weed out a few of the *wrong* courses—courses that had YOUTUBE videos of the work being done with the horse in a round pen.

The videos were the most confusing thing I had ever seen. The horse was confused too! The therapist in the video was trying to show leadership, but the horse had no respect for her. He was pushy and looking for treats, and it was obvious the woman had no idea how to be the leader. If I'd taken that course and done that to my horses, they would have hated me! So, I kept looking and I found the right course in Wisconsin with Pam Kachelmeier. I began the online webinar classes and then flew three months later to attend a four-day hands-on class with the rest of the class and Pam and her horses. It was amazing!

Pam is a therapist, but her course is for coaches and I was already a life coach. I just needed the education to learn to partner with the horses! I made new friends and colleagues. I had to give a lesson in front of the class, and I was told I was a natural healer. I had no idea how this new path would play out, but it gave me so much to take home and use in my practice. It took about a year to get that certification and now, here I am!!

You just never know who or what will come into your life and change it!! I now love myself to death!! I am an amazing person, I have three thriving older children, and I am a life coach because of my past experiences. It all made sense. That is why I had to go through all my anger and sadness – my issues with my mother and family. I finally got it!

I now live my life in consciousness. As an empath, I can feel what is going on inside people and though sometimes it is heavy and exhausting for me, I am so grateful because any different step could have led me elsewhere. This is where I belong and guess what? My son is now clean and sober! I have an awesome relationship with my kids, and my own mother told me before she died, "Gina, you are a much better mother than I ever was." I have made peace with my life.

Looking back, that parent's exercise in Utah was my bottom. We all need to hit our bottom at some point as the start of our healing. We must go through the pain to get to the point that we ask it to stop and then do something about stopping it! It takes courage and determination, but it's so worth it!

Blue and my son celebrating Robert's four years clean and sober with a fun bareback ride at my farm.

Respect the Ride

"Riding, like life, doesn't have to be perfect to be wonderful!"—Author unknown

Whips. Tie downs. Spurs. Bits. These are all common tools for getting horses to do what we want. Terms like "breaking" a horse to be ridden is so common, too, we may not even think to ask, "Why would anyone want to 'break' a horse?"

The way of thinking behind this terminology and these behavioral aids may be the "norm" when it comes to horseback riding, but they aren't respectful to the horse. It pays to remember; horses are prey animals. When a wildcat attacks a horse, it goes for the horse's neck first to bring it down and then leaps on its back to finish the kill. Yet, when we ride a horse, we are asking the horse to let us do similar things. Think about it! We put a bit in its mouth, put reins around its neck, strap on a heavy leather saddle on its back, and climb aboard. And it lets us! It should be obvious that this immense level of trust they give us to ride on their backs deserves an immense amount of respect from us in return. Sadly, this isn't obvious to many. Instead, so many riders and trainers use whips, spurs, tie downs, restraints, metal mouth bits, and other painful behavioral aids that are not respectful of the horse.

As if this isn't bad enough, I've witnessed people riding horses while drunk, stinking of cigarettes and meat, being loud, and acting like jerks in the saddle, yanking the bit and pulling the reins, hitting and yelling at the horse, and calling it "stupid." This raucous, disrespectful behavior is disgusting.

It's an honor that a horse lets someone on its back at all. Some horses will tolerate a rider's bad behavior, but some horses won't and will buck the rider clear off—and that person would deserve it.

Save the Horses is a wonderful equine rescue facility in Georgia. It's founder, Cheryl, works tirelessly to rehabilitate the abused and neglected horses that come into her care. One day while I was visiting her barn, Cheryl told me a sad, horrific story about a horse named Trudy.

Trudy was an older mare who had been owned by two bullies who decided to one day jump on her back and be "cowboys."

When they began to hit her, Trudy bucked them off. The men decided to get even with her and wrapped Trudy in barbed wire and dragged her behind their truck. I have no words for this level of soulless cruelty.

Trudy went to live with Cheryl after someone witnessed this abuse. It's hard to know what other abuses Trudy had endured in her life. She had a much better life at the rescue but by that point, Trudy had gone blind.

The day I met this amazing mare, I could feel her sadness and it affected me deeply. She was a kind horse, but she had a broken heart. She lived with Cheryl for a few years before she died. The good thing is Trudy's last years were spent with someone loving and kind, but nothing could rectify the abuse she endured at the hands of horrible humans. Thankfully, not all stories are this severe. But we believe people can treat their horses unfairly and abusively without realizing they are, simply because they are following the "norm."

The way you handle your horse is a special relationship between you both. Which riding style you prefer doesn't matter nearly as much as the relationship you share with your horse and the respect you give him or her. I have seen kids learn little more than how to saddle the horse before climbing up to ride or jump. The problem is they lack respect for their equine partner. No one taught them how to pause and take time to create a relationship with the horse first.

They were asking the horse to work for them, not with them. A horse is not a tractor or a truck, and it should never be used and then put away. A horse should be deemed a partner worthy of respect and relationship. People can focus too much on proper horseback riding form. While this may be important for the safety of horse and rider, it's equally important to take the time to develop a partnership and learn to listen to the horse.

"When I hear somebody talk about a horse or a cow being stupid, I figure it's a sure sign that the animal has somehow outfoxed them."—Tom Dorrance

In our experience as riders and equine-assisted coaches, we know the value of taking the time to do hours of groundwork with a horse before we ever attempt to ride. Through groundwork, we learn to know the horse and understand him or her.

A bond is created, and our chance of getting bucked off the horse for being disrespectful drastically decreases. When your horse is happy and trusts you, you will have a friend for life. And no behavioral aids like bits, spurs, whips, and tie-downs will be necessary. Trust us on this one.

From the Heart of Horses—Listen and You'll Learn

"I know that you believe you understand what you think I said, but I am not sure you realize that what you heard is not what I meant."—Tom Dorrance

No horse's background is the same. Horses have their own history just like us—some healthy, some traumatic. I also know that not all horses act like mine do. But at their core, horses are horses, and even a wild, feral horse or someone else's horse can teach you something about yourself. That is, if you are willing to listen.

A lot of talk goes on about people being horse whispers. As a matter of fact, one of my favorite movies is called *The Horse Whisperer.* It stars Robert Redford and Scarlett Johansson. It's the story of a young girl who had been involved in a horrific accident on horseback when a semi, driving on slippery iced roads, cannot stop and seriously injures Scarlett and her horse, Pilgrim, and kills her best friend and her horse. The movie is intense, but the lessons about rehabbing the horse and the rider are highly valuable.

(It is worth noting that Buck Brannaman, one of our equine expert heroes, whom we frequently quote in this book, was the actual inspiration for Redford's character, Tom Booker, in the movie, as well as in the Nicholas Evans book on which it is based.)

Where most people might be inclined to put down the injured animal, thinking he will never be the same, through *whispering, or listening,* Booker (played by Robert Redford) restores the horse's belief in himself. Similarly, he teaches his young rider, who is now missing a leg, how to gain her confidence back—to literally "get back in the saddle" and metaphorically move on with her life. She does and the bond between Pilgrim and her becomes stronger than ever.

That is the healing that a horse can give us, and they do so out of loyalty and devotion. The horse is the most noble of companions, and even when you give up on yourself, the horse is there to remind you that he hasn't. We can and should, in turn, offer that kind of healing to a horse in need as well.

Debra and I are horse listeners. We hear them when they tell us they are ill or hurt. We hear them when something scares them. We also listen when they just want to hang out with us or be with their friends and graze on the sweet green grass under the shade trees.

If Debra and I have a special understanding of horses, it's because we listen, watch, and learn from them. We have learned how they interact with each other and how they play and live within their small or large herds.

"All I want is the wind in my hair, to face the fear but not feel scared. ...I wanna open up my heart, tell him how I feel ... wish I could recklessly love, like I'm longing to. I wanna run with the wild horses."—Natasha Bedingfield, Wild Horses

One of my very favorite things to do is to watch a herd of wild horses run. My husband once took me to Cumberland

Island for my birthday for an entire weekend of just watching the wild horses. To date, it was my best birthday ever! As the story goes, Spanish Conquistadors brought the wild horses to Cumberland island sometime around the 1600s. Then, left alone by the property owners of Cumberland Island, they eventually became feral and learned to survive on their own.

A functional band of horses requires all members of the band (aka "herd") to be in sync with each other and their environment. His or her very survival depends on each member doing his or her part. Because of this, bonding comes naturally to horses. Trust is part of bonding. I love to implement the herd mentality in working with clients. I explain how the herd works and that it is a tough mare that leads it. A few of the men are a little put off at the thought of a female running things, but it is like that a lot in nature.

Herds of elephants (who are related to horses) are matriarchal. Both male emus and penguins hatch the eggs and raise the chicks. Female lions are the fearless hunters for their prides. The list goes on and on among our animal brothers and sisters. To a horse, the herd is paramount. It is their community and their family. The horse is a very social creature.

If you buy one, you should buy two because they really do not enjoy being alone. For a human to enter a horse's world, there must be trust. Like a herd dynamic, human and horse must have each other's back to ensure the safety and wellbeing of both. Food, shelter, security, and emotional and physical safety are essential to the horse. This hierarchy of needs is not much different humans. Unfortunately, since humans are at the top of the food chain, we can be defined as a "predator." For predator and prey to coexist, respect must exist. Respect is an act of love.

A strong trust bond entails healthy boundaries, structure, responsibilities, and genuine care and concern for the other party's welfare. And yes, horses do this with each other. I've seen a horse protect a disabled herd member by making other horses keep their distance.

Communication is another element in bonding. How do you and your horse communicate with each other? The obvious limitations between two different species can be overcome with a willingness to understand the other. What are your needs? What are my needs? What do I expect from you, and what do you expect from me?

Time spent grooming, which horses do with each other in the herd, is a great way to build that bond. In my time at the SPCA (Society for the Prevention of Cruelty to Animals) as an equine specialist, I witnessed horses that were edgy and nervous while being groomed by one client but who would fall asleep while being groomed by the next one.

How is your horse responding under your or your client's touch? I really pay attention to how they respond when being groomed by a client. I find that handing the client a brush and asking them to brush the horse will oftentimes scare them, or they may be taken aback at how basic an exercise I have suggested.

As they begin to groom the horse, however, their mood changes. They begin to relax and so does my horse. This is a great time for the client to start opening up. I teach them to pick up my horse's feet, especially if we are dealing with fear. The big "WHAT?" is when I tell them to walk behind my horse! I tell them to be calm and just let the horse know they are behind him.

It can sometimes take up to twenty minutes for them to get up their courage. After twenty minutes or so of constantly stroking my horse, they finally acquiesce. With a long, extended arm and quick pace, they circle the horse at a distance. I start laughing inside because I know this game and so does my horse. Then I tell them, "Good job – do it again." They often look at me like I've lost my mind. By the fifth or sixth time, though, they usually have conquered most of their fear. It's a great technique for building trust with someone that has zero.

I also teach them a lot of the horse's body language. Humans have lost some of our body-language-reading skills—living once-removed, virtual lives on computers or texting—and grooming a horse is a great way to get that back.

When I work with clients that have no or little horse experience, they need to overcome the obstacles to which their disbelief leads them. People think my horses are trained to do what they do in sessions. They are not. I allow the horse to just be with the client and to do what they feel they have to do. I am always there nearby to oversee and guide the client. I am as present as the horse, and that is why we work together so well. They know what we are doing; they know we are partners.

When you're with your horse, stay in the moment. Don't get on your phone. Don't be drunk or high. And if you're in a bad mood, just be honest about it. You can say, "Hey, buddy, I'm in a rotten mood right now, but is it okay if we hang out and I brush you for a little while?" You'll most likely find your horse will say, "Okay, come on, friend. I can help you." And in the process, your heart rate will lower, and your mood will mellow out to the rhythm of the brushing.

I do this as I am walking to my barn: before I walk in, I check my attitude and intentions at the door. Although, no matter what I'm feeling, the minute I walk into the barn and I see one or both of my boys standing there watching me, I cannot help but get a big smile on my face as I walk over to and pet them both. I love them so much and that is the intention and energy I want them to pick up on. I want them to know I am happy to be with them, and we can have fun and do some work or do nothing—either way, I'm happy just to be with them.

Gina in 2012 at Cumberland Island for her birthday. These horses are true feral horses and their ancestors were brought over by the Carnegie family in 1880. After the entire family left the island in the 1900's, the horses were left by their mistress, Mrs.Carnegie, to roam and live free.

Gina in 2012 at Cumberland Island practicing a "whispering" technique in just sitting down and letting the horse approach you. This is another feral horse and he is noticing Gina and thinking about approaching. Unfortunately, a very loud observer came running up behind Gina and the horse took off running.

He Knew I was coming, so He Waited— Dodger's Story

The language of friendship is not words but meaning—
Henry David Thoreau

When I first met my rescue horse, Dodger, I was visiting my longtime broadcasting friend Roy in Miami, Florida. Roy is like a brother to me, and my husband and he are good friends. I was down for a quick visit to see my daughter Talia and met up with Roy for dinner and a day of riding his horses. It was a beautiful sunny day and after breakfast at Roy's favorite place to eat, Waffle House, we decided to go visit the horses at the SPCA in Homestead. Roy is the treasurer, and I had volunteered to work with them several years ago.

We drove the 32 miles to the SPCA. I just wanted to visit; I wasn't going to adopt a horse. The timing was wrong for that, as my husband and I had just bought a small farm on four acres with a house that a required a foundation-to-roof rehab, plus we had to build a barn and put up fencing. But the Universe had shown me many times to be careful what I wish for because it may arrive whether I'm ready for it or not!

The SPCA was a haven for 47 rescue horses of just about every size and breed you could imagine. It's sad when people throw animals away like garbage, but thankfully there are amazing rescues like the SPCA, ASPCA, humane societies and privately run 501(c)(3)'s that rescue horses that have been abused, neglected, and/or abandoned.

We met up with Laurie, the founder of the SPCA, at the property and she gave Roy and me a tour of the facility. As we walked along the long rows of stalls, I told Laurie I wasn't really looking for a horse yet, but if I found a Quarter horse (a breed I think of as the Labrador retriever of the horse world), I might be interested. On the tour, I saw a bunch of mini ponies and some large horses but no quarter horses.

After we had walked the entire property, casually looking around, we returned to the barn, and I stopped in front of a stall and casually rested my arm on top of the stall door. Suddenly, my arm was pushed off!

I turned to look at what prankster had done this and, standing right in front of me, was a brown horse with a white star on his forehead. I laughed and put my arm back on his stall door; he pushed it off again.

Laurie laughed and told me that he was a Morgan horse and very smart. She said she'd never seen him interact like that with anyone before. I was curious. I asked her if I could walk into the stall to see him. I also asked him if that was okay. Laurie warned me to be careful because he was still considered a little wild and didn't seem to trust many people. They had named him Dodger because, like an untrained horse, he would dodge everyone to avoid being caught.

I walked toward the back of his stall near a big window and started talking to him. I turned to look out the window, and then a beautiful thing happened—Dodger turned around, too, and we stood side-by-side looking outside through his window. I wish I had a photo of that moment.

The energy in the stall was very calm, but the energy I sensed from Dodger himself was eager and anxious. The rescue was a wonderful place, but he wanted to leave. He wanted a home of his own. I kept hearing the words: "Now! I want to leave now. Take me with you."

At that time, I hadn't been around horses for several years, and feeling a horse's energy was a new sensation of which I was just becoming aware. I used to feel it as a kid when I was around horses, but my intuition knew this is what Dodger was saying, and I sensed there was something special about him.

After I left the rescue that day, I kept thinking about Dodger. I wanted to grant his wish but just wasn't sure. I was hoping for a blue roan Quarter Horse, but here was this frisky Morgan asking to come home with me.

What is more, Dodger's story wrenched my heart. When I had asked about his history, the SPCA folks told me a harrowing story. From what they could guess, Dodger most likely had once had a home with someone who was good to him and trained him well, but somewhere along the way, he was sold to a neglectful, cruel owner who later loaded this beautiful horse into a trailer and hauled him out to the Everglades where he was dumped and left for dead.

Yes, you read that right. He was abandoned in the Everglades with alligators, wild dog packs, and pythons— not to mention having to survive severe storms, isolation, and starvation. This once-domesticated horse that had depended on people to meet his needs was let down by humans in such a way that he had to revert to his primal roots and become feral.

Can you even imagine the stress, hunger, and fear this poor horse experienced? To be alone for so long and not have at least one other horse there to be on guard if Dodger wanted to lie down and sleep had to be exhausting and traumatic.

He survived, barely, all alone in those dangerous Everglades for almost two years before someone spotted him and alerted the SPCA. Laura and her team immediately started searching for him.

When they found him, Dodger (who had no name then) was emaciated and his eyes were wild with terror. They had a difficult time catching him because of his fear and mistrust of humans. It took several hours to get him onto the trailer. With hay, treats, and a lot of patience, they were finally able to convince Dodger he was safe enough to load up and take back to the farm.

He was placed in rehab with regular feeding and vet care and finally gained his weight and health back. He was thirteen years old, which is considered middle-aged for a horse, and he was wild and rough. The SPCA folks did what they could to get him around people again, and he was making some progress by the time I came along.

Could you imagine going through all of this? This horse's courage and heart still astonish me. And the fact that Dodger would give a human one more chance and choose ME to be that human is a gift I can't describe. But perhaps he saw that I was a lot like him. Maybe he sensed I'd gone through abuse and disappointments, too, and for a long time, lived in survival mode on my own. Perhaps he saw the broken and terrified parts of me I was still in the process of healing. And maybe he saw my courage, too. Maybe he felt we could help each other.

The night after I met him, all I did was dream about that silly prankster horse. When I woke up in the morning, I knew I had to go get him. I started the adoption process and, five days later, Dodger was mine.

I knew I was helping Dodger by adopting him, but I had no idea how much this horse would change my life. So many new things were about to come my way because of him: new paths, new lessons, new friends, and new realizations within myself I never could have predicted.

When I had been approved to adopt him, silence engulfed me. I was thrilled that I had a horse again. It felt so good. But, at the same time, I was nervous. Now what? Not being quite ready (as I said, we had a barn to raise and fences to install at our property—urgently now), I opted to send Dodger to a trainer that Laurie recommended. He went to learn how to be a domesticated and trained horse again before coming to Georgia to live with me.

Dodger was there for eight weeks while I prepared for his arrival. During this time, the trainer worked with Dodger to overcome his fear of noises, wind, hats, being bathed, and, especially, his fear of being ridden. Dodger was fearful of pretty much everything, but with good reason. His fear was imbedded within him. I had no idea how long it would actually take to help him overcome it. I knew I had a big job in front of me and so did Dodger.

Dodger may have chosen me to adopt him, but when it came to him fully trusting me, he made me earn it. I learned a lot about patience, a skill of which I have never had much. I learned it with Dodger though because he didn't give me much of a choice otherwise! I had to be patient and understanding until that horse really was sure he could trust me and that I wasn't going to hurt him.

One of my greatest hopes is that people realize how special it is to have an animal trust you. They are sentient and capable of many emotions like humans. They bond with their babies, they worry, they defend, they nurture, they play, and they love. Once I connected with Dodger, I began living more in consciousness. My mind and heart were wide open because of this gorgeous soul that knew we had purpose together.

The amazing thing is he already knew this. I had to learn from him, and I discovered we are all one. We are all connected—from the smallest bug to the largest mammal to rocks, plants, and flowers. Any scientist or DNA specialist can show you how closely related we genetically are to these some of these creatures, some within a mere three DNA points.

All horses are amazing. But, for me, there's something extra special about a rescue horse. And I can honestly say I never expected to have one! But that's how my life was supposed to unfold. Rescue horses are grateful. They may not show it like a dog will but in time as you build that connection with the horse, they will let you know.

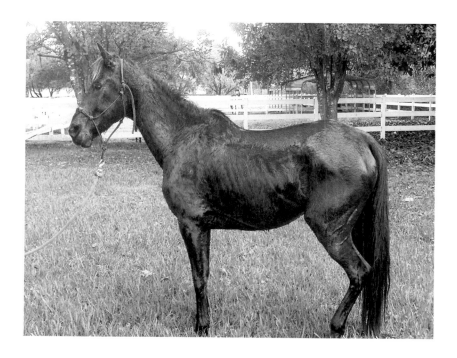

Dodger had been found abandoned and starving in the Everglades of Florida.
They estimate he had been trying to survive for about two years before
someone reported a lost starving horse loose in the Glades.

Dodger's Journey Back to Himself

"Believe in your horse so your horse can believe in you."—Ray Hunt

Eight weeks later, in June of 2017, Dodger arrived in Georgia. The fencing at our farm still wasn't done, so I arranged to board him at a barn not too far away so I could see him every day. I hadn't seen Dodger in two months, and I had only seen him twice before at the SPCA barn.

As I watched him walk off the trailer, I felt strong emotions. I felt love for this horse, and I felt excitement about him finally being with me, but I also felt fear about how much faith he was putting in me. I didn't want to let him down. I took his lead rope and stood with him for a few minutes, hoping he remembered me.

The farm was green and alive with the sounds of singing birds and whinnying horses. Enormous trees surrounded us. Dodger and I were the new kids at the barn. Riding him was the furthest thing from my mind. We were going to do a lot of groundwork and take time to get to know each other. We were going to take time to build trust and a friendship.

After a few minutes, we walked slowly to his new pasture. I walked us through the gate and gave him an apple. Dodger ate that apple like he had never tasted one before. It was adorable to watch him enjoy it so much. He ate the whole thing and had a ton of juice and bubbly froth all over his mouth. He was like a toddler with his first cookie, and I was already totally in love with him.

I took off the halter and lead rope and let him go. He had been mostly in a stall since his rescue. Dodger held up his head, pricked his ears and began snorting as he trotted up and down the fence, neighing. His tail was held high and he looked so majestic. How could anyone have thrown away this gorgeous creature?

I gave Dodger two days to settle in and get to know his pasture mate, a Quarter Horse named Louie who belonged to an older woman that had had him for years.

He was a bit older but very sound, and I thought he'd make a good pasture mate for Dodger. And then our work began.

Although I knew he had gone through hard times, I wasn't going to insult his dignity by babying him. I had to start all over with him. I had no bridle, saddle, or halter and with him being afraid of most everything, using the right tack was imperative. I ended up purchasing a rope-training halter, the kind with knots on it. (Debra and I make jokes about those other fancier halters. We call them "creek halters" because they belong in the bottom of a creek!)

I ordered a saddle and bought him a bridle with a training snaffle bit—the most common type of bit used while riding horses. I had no idea where to begin as it had been years since I had a horse. I went to halter Dodger in his pasture and he took off running. Boy, he was fast! And he was funny, too. To this day, he's probably the smartest horse I have ever had. When Dodger saw me coming, he would hide behind Louie. Then, as I approached Louie, Dodger would walk backwards to go to the other side of his friend. Then Dodger would take off running.

"Okay, Dodger", I laughed, "If you want to run from me, then let's run." I chased him around the pasture pushing him forward and getting his feet moving. Then he would go behind a tree and peek around the tree to see if I could see him. (You had to laugh at how smart he was!) Again I would chase him. The idea was to show him that being with me was better than running and working. Of course, he finally got tired and stood snorting and trying to defy me but eventually, he walked up to me and allowed me to put on the halter. We were doing the groundwork. We were taking the time.

I stood with him for a few minutes petting him and speaking to him gently.

He started licking his lips and then I knew he was thinking and learning: licking and chewing is a positive sign of a horse starting to "get it."

Then we would head into the round pen to do some more groundwork. A round pen is a circular arena typically about thirty to sixty feet in circumference. It's a smaller arena that allows the horse to move but keep him close enough to you to have some contact and help him hook on to you. By pushing him forward and getting his feet moving, I am imitating the herd mentality. The older mare that leads the herd does this to establish leadership.

Speaking in his language, that is, the language of the herd, he understood that I was making him respect me and asking him to follow me, like he would if he were in a herd of horses. Once you establish leadership, it's a natural thing that a horse will follow you because you have become the leader of his herd. If you are not a capable leader, then the horse has no choice but to do what he thinks is necessary for him to survive. That is; he will lead and *you* will be treated like one the herd.

So, once I got his respect by getting his feet moving, that is, running, he eventually let me know he was ready and came into the middle of the ring and faced me with his two eyes looking right at me. Then I knew he had joined my herd and was ready to learn from me.

Though I'd established myself as the "lead mare," getting him to hook on to me took some time. He would run frantically in the round pen, thrashing and whinnying for help. He snorted and tossed his head, and it scared me at first to watch him, but this was a process for both of us. For me, it was gaining the courage and confidence within myself and being able to listen to him.

Learning to trust me was his challenge. He had to see me as a good leader and luckily, I had shown him I was capable of the job. Today, Dodger sees me when I walk outside toward the pasture, and when I whistle; he raises his head and walks right to me. His warm black eyes have love and friendship in them. He is playful and very, very happy!

After about three weeks of all groundwork with him in the round pen, I decided it was time to ride him. The Western saddle I ordered had arrived, and I put him in the arena, saddled him up, and gave it a go. He was okay with the mounting, but as soon as I tried to canter him, he took off, started bucking, and I jumped off!

As I lay on the ground with my face in the dirt, Dodger turned around and looked at me as if to say, "What the heck just happened?" I got back on and we walked, but I decided I needed some help. That's when I met Dusty, my equine guru.

Some may feel it's best to do everything yourself; I see nothing wrong with hiring an expert if you can. Dodger was a rescue and had some quirks other horses may not. There were going to be triggers that could be set off and if I wasn't careful, Dodger or I could get seriously hurt.

The first time I spoke to Dusty over the phone, he told me he was going to talk to my horse and discuss what was going on with him and what was expected of him. I thought, "Far out, he's going to talk to my horse." When Dusty showed up at the barn, his truck had a license plate that said, "COEXIST." I thought that was a exceptionally good sign. I led Dodger out and Dusty watched closely to see what Dodger might tell him.

Dusty talked to Dodger. He said Dodger told him he was scared and didn't want to be in trouble, but he didn't understand what he was supposed to do. Dusty convinced him to trust us and in doing so, everything would be okay.

Together, we worked with him in the arena trying to build his confidence.

After the first few days of working with Dodger, Dusty and I concluded that my horse needed a lot more work. He was not safe to take into any situation that was loud or had a lot of people. He needed a lot more confidence building.

Dusty had him do things that helped build his confidence. We had Dodger walk over a pile of loose boards (that were safe for him to walk on). I brought balloons, flags, garbage can lids and other distracting or noisy objects. We would startle him with these noises in the round pen. He would run and show the whites of his eyes until he finally felt he was safe and didn't have to be afraid. Scaring your horse in incremental exercises until he's no longer afraid anymore is the best way to help him overcome fear and get more confident.

It's like the systematic desensitization technique used with people with phobias. It doesn't mean you terrorize him though. There is a fine line between confidence building and abuse.

This applies to clients as well. I have found that presenting challenges to a client and pushing them to "walk through the fire" is when transformation truly happens.

 It is all about letting go and taking that leap of faith. It's utilizing pressure and release, just like I use on the horses. The pressure is what scares us, but it also helps us face and confront those fears and doubts. The release is what happens naturally as you look back and realize you have just succeeded at doing what you once thought impossible.

Dodger learned confidence and to trust when pressure, release, and reward were applied. Now, he is the sweetest most playful and trusting horse. Dodger is also my busiest equine coach, and he loves the women and children! Now, he knows his job and he knows he is great at it!

Dodger finally recovered thanks to the SPCA! Notice the look in his eyes. He looked like he had given up in his Intake picture. Now he looks healthy and hopeful. I adopted him about one year after this picture was taken in 2014.

You've Got to Have Friends

"If you want a stable friendship, get a horse." — *Author unknown*

Once I'd brought Dodger to my farm and a few months of our working together had passed, I had made great progress with Dodger. But I knew he was lonely and that I had to find a companion for him.

I decided to travel back to Miami, where I'd originally found Dodger. During that time, I had gone riding again with my friend Roy. While at his barn where he boarded his three horses, there was a gorgeous quarter horse mare named Penny. The poor thing was locked in her stall all day and night. She was desperate to get out and graze, but her owner never showed up to visit or ride her. Penny would pace back and forth, and anyone or anything that came by her window would bring her right up it to socialize and try to convince them to let her out.

On that Saturday while riding in the arena on Roy's horse, Bubba, I inquired about Penny. She was for sale! I took her out and worked her in the round pen, and she joined up quickly with me. She was anxious, but I got her calmed down and did a bit of groundwork with her for about an hour. At the end of that hour, she was much calmer and we had connected. She was so gorgeous, and I knew Dodger would love her. But the owner seemed unsure of the price or whether even to sell her or not, so I walked away from her, disappointed but not giving up.

This is where manifestation comes into play. I meditated a lot on finding the right horse for Dodger and me. On the way home, my friend Juan gave me a call.
I had long been looking to adopt a blue roan quarter horse. My friend Juan had adopted one a few years back, and I always told him that if he ever needed to give him up, I wanted him! Blue was a Hancock blue breeding stallion with an amazing personality—he was so much fun!

The Blue Roan Quarter Horse is a unique color of blue. He is a roan with white speckled hairs throughout his black coat, which looks grey in some lighting and truly blue in other. They are very smart and famous for being great cattle horses. One of Blue's prior owners got a few blue roan stallions, including Blue, and then decided they would be better breeders if he starved them!

Luckily, these stallions were rescued, and Juan adopted Blue—a $12,000 stallion that was starving and who had been originally bought strictly to make money. Once he got Blue healthy again, he trained him to be ridden, gelded him (castrated him) to make him better behaved and easier to control, and Blue became a green-level reigning champion.

Juan had trained him for a reining competition. His task was to run into the ring as fast as he could, come to a sliding stop, and then, on cue, spin around in a circle until he was cued to stop and run back out the arena. Whoever had the fastest time won. Blue won the championship for his size and weight!

So, when Juan called and told me he was going through a divorce and needed to re-home Blue, I jumped at the opportunity. I brought that horse home about a month later, right before Thanksgiving weekend.

When Blue arrived, it was a cold fall night. We were all sitting out around the big fire pit in our yard. Our kids were up visiting and my dear friend Dusty had joined us for Thanksgiving dinner.

The big horse trailer pulled into our long driveway, and I knew inside that trailer was my dream horse. I'd had blue roan on the brain for months. I had looked at and ridden a few and I had meditated on manifesting a blue roan quarter horse. Now, the Universe had brought me one. Not just any blue roan, but the one I had wanted for years. And he was free—a gift! All I had to do was take him because a friend couldn't take care of him anymore.

The big trailer doors opened and the transporter handed me Blue's winter blanket. Coming from Florida, he had no winter hair to keep him warm, and the temperature was about 45 degrees outside. I took the lead rope and led him out of the trailer. He was huge! I put the blanket on him and gave him a treat. I welcomed him to his new home.

Everyone was in awe of how majestic and gorgeous he was.

He took his head and pushed me a bit and I smiled and led him to his stall right next to Dodger. Dodger was so happy, he turned around and looked me in the eye and said, "Thank you."

It didn't take as long for me to get to know Blue, but I did move just as slow as I had with Dodger. He was a lot bigger than Dodger and could be ridden but, honestly, his size was intimidating. I thought "Oh boy, I've got more to learn about myself, and I guess Blue is here to teach me more." Dusty and I spent about three weeks working with Blue.

We decided Blue seemed calm and confident and certainly not spooked easily. So, we decided it was time to take the two horses out on the trail.

I had never taken Dodger to ride on the trails—ever! I had no idea if he would scream in the trailer or bolt and run away when unloaded. Maybe he would take off running when on the trails. It was a risk, but Dusty was planning on riding Dodger and I was to ride Blue.

Dodger was a little nervous but calmed down being next to Blue in the trailer.
We drove to Kennesaw State Park and unloaded them slowly, giving them time to look around and settle. We really took our time, and I think it made all the difference.

At last, the saddles were on the horses, water bottles and some treats were in the saddlebags, and we were ready to go.

Mounting up, we turned and began walking the horses down the unknown path. And then the most unexpected, amazing thing happened. Dodger took the lead—and Blue let him. Dodger held his head beautifully, tail up, ears pricked and walked so proudly and regally. We couldn't believe it!

In that moment, I saw that all the handling, touching, supporting, and patience we'd shown him were paying off for this once-terrified horse. Dodger had good manners and confidence! He had been allowed to be a horse, make a supportive equine friend, and develop a relationship with a human. Dodger trusted me, and I was so happy to finally see it.

My son Antonio, Dusty and I going out for our first ride with Blue at Kennesaw Mountain Park. Dodger is right behind Blue 2016

Angels and Horses and Bad Apples

"The horse. Here is nobility without conceit, friendship without envy, beauty without vanity. A willing servant yet never a slave." - Ronald Duncan

When clients come to coaching sessions at my farm, they are usually excited to know that at some point in our sessions together, we will partner with the horses. I often warn some of the "high maintenance" types to approach them slowly, however soon after their approach and the Ego shows up, my horses let me know it and they'll let the client know it as well!

Though most of my clients are amazing, I have had one or two "bad apples" here. One night we were hosting a fire walk for a small group and one client who believed himself to be a "horse whisperer" (and believed it enough to say it out loud) approached Blue. As soon as my horse saw the man walking toward him, he stopped grazing and walked right past him.

My client looked stunned. He decided to try again. Blue did the same thing. This guy approached Blue with that typical cowboy "I'm the boss of you" ego thing going on and wasn't interested in introducing himself and getting to know Blue at all. He was sure my horse would fall all over him. He was putting on an egotistical front and wasn't being real.

If we aren't real with our horses, we will get ignored or worse — kicked, bitten or thrown off. I think the same thing happens to human relationships when you encounter someone you know is leading with (or hiding behind) ego and isn't being real.

Ego can be found in all circles and all walks of life. We may know people who talk about how big their house is, the new car they drive, and where they went to college. But there can also be ego in how minimalist, spiritual, or eco-conscious we try to be, or think we are. These things in and of themselves aren't bad (usually). But it can become a hindrance when we hide behind them and depend on to make us feel important.

Horses have helped me to strip away layers of what I used to carry around to feel like "someone." They have helped become more authentic, and I'm happier than I've ever been! Being authentic means learning to be OK with the real version of who you are. It means letting go of worrying about what people think and stop trying to prove to them that you're worthy.

Horses are just what they are – no fluff. They don't try to impress each other. They don't put off eating that patch of grass until tomorrow. And they don't wimp out on disciplining herd members because they are afraid of a horse disliking them. I wish more people could live like that. Does this sound like you? Who is the Authentic You? Once you strip away the layers of inauthenticity in your life, it's so freeing. Everything feels possible!

The horse is the most honest thing you will ever have in your life. Not even a dog is this honest. A dog will love you even if you are mean to it. He may not trust you but will become submissive at the first attempt to ask forgiveness. A horse doesn't care like this. Their world is one of respect and rank and survival. The more authentic you can be with your horse, the better relationship you will have with him. A horse is one of the most noble and most loyal of all creatures. They are also extremely intelligent. If you have a friend in your horse, you have the best friend you will ever have.

A friend of mine once told me an incredibly sad story of how his wife died. He was so distraught. She had died of Cancer and though the months of her time left turned into weeks and then into days and finally, into hours, he let her go.

What surprised him was he couldn't cry. He said it felt as though it was locked inside of him with no way out. Finally, about two weeks after the funeral, he found enough strength to take his horse out for an overdue and much needed ride.

As he rode through the field, he felt like he needed to just stop and get off his horse.

As he did, he knelt onto the ground right beside his horse. All at once, the tears started and just wouldn't stop. Right then, his horse (his trusted friend) reached his neck around my friend's shoulder and pulled him to his chest. His horse just held him there for what seemed an eternity. My friend needed that hug so badly and his horse knew it.

It was the release of sadness and pain that needed to be released. His horse just knew. It is a testament as to how strong their connection was. As the horse understood what my friend needed at that very moment and with no hesitation or worry about being scolded, he knew it was ok.

How many times have you just spent time with your horse asking him to do nothing? What about just going into the barn and giving him a treat just because he's a good horse? You have no idea how much that means to them.

There are many moments like this that happens between rider and horse. I wish more people would stop worrying so much about competing and showing and whether their horse is holding his head in the perfect position for the judges. The horse is a healer if we are willing to believe that they can and more importantly, they want to.

Coaching with Children: Katie and Clarice

"Some of my best friends never say a word to me." –
Author unknown

I work with clients of different ages, backgrounds and experiences, but without fail the ones who breaks my heart the most are the children. A few years ago, a female Rebecca came to me for help with her 9-year-old daughter, Katie. Katie's parents had recently divorced, and her father was an alcoholic who would drink until he blacked out and would not feed Katie and her 5-year-old sister when they visited him for the weekend. Katie was sad and angry and needed help. I let her mother know that, as a life coach, I couldn't testify for her in court to try to get his custody revoked, but I would do what I could to help her little girl.

Acting out of her trauma, Katie had been hitting her little sister and yelling at her mother; at times she would go long bouts without speaking and although Katie was seeing a pediatric therapist, it wasn't helping. I decided to ask Dodger to help me work with this little girl. I meditated before she arrived so I would be peaceful and open for her. I had healed my own abusive childhood many years ago with my alcoholic mother and knew that being able to empathize with how Katie felt would be helpful.

Dodger had been waiting for her since early this morning. I told him she was coming, and he knew he had a special job that morning – to reach this little girl's closed-off heart and help her to believe in her worth despite her drunken father's abusive, neglectful choices.

Her hopeful mother drove to my farm and passed my big black gate with the *Tree of Life* symbol nailed onto the front of the wide wooden door.

Dodger pricked up his ears. As I approached him and put on his rope halter and lead him out of the barn, Katie stepped out of her mother's SUV and looked across the pasture. I could already see the sadness in her eyes. Dodger could too. He watched her walk towards us. She needed him and he was ready. He understood her heartbreak, sadness, confusion and rage. Katie was angry that her parents were no longer together, and that she was abandoned by her father, forced to look out for herself and her little sister when she should have been protected. Dodger experienced similar when he was fighting for his life in the Everglades after being heartlessly abandoned there to fend for himself.

I approached their car and hugged her mom and then reached down to the girls and hugged them too. I could feel the pain and confusion. It broke my heart.

Katie and I walked to Dodger and went into the round pen and I handed Katie the lead rope and taught her how to hold it properly – never wrapping it around her hand, wrist or arm. Dodger lowered his head and what happened next was magical. I instructed her to begin walking in the round pen with him. She was holding the lead rope on her own and I asked her to start telling Dodger about her day. I wanted to see if she would open up to him.

Dodger is very gentle and loves children. He walked with his head lowered, level to her height, and had one ear turned toward her, listening as she spoke. She started a simple conversation with him. She walked back to me with Dodger's lead rope in her hand and looked at me. She looked angry and sad at the same time. I understood.

I asked her if she felt comfortable talking about her dad yet. She says "No, not yet." I respected that and sent her walking with Dodger again in the round pen. As she is walking, I ask her to stop every few minutes and gave her instructions: "Tell Dodger what you did in school today." She did and begins walking again. "Stop," I tell her. "Now, tell Dodger what you are most afraid off." She told him like a whispered secret and then started walking again. "Stop", I say again. Now tell Dodger what you're sad about. She stops walking him and she starts talking about her dad. She continues walking and I say "Stop" one more time.

 "Tell him a joke." She looks at me and giggles then does. I ask her, "Did he listen to you?"

"Yes," she giggled again

"Did he laugh at you?", I asked.

"No", she said, with a giggle and then a smile.

"Do you feel you can trust Dodger?" I asked.

"Yes", she said.

I told her to bring Dodger into the barn where she could brush him. She did and I could feel her beginning to relax. No one was being cruel or unfair to her. It was just she and Dodger in a safe space, with me as the guide. After brushing Dodger, she turned to me and said," I'm ready to talk about my Daddy now." This was Katie's first time talking about her feelings about her dad. And although she couldn't tell her dad directly how she was feeling, because he was in denial about his drinking problem, Dodger was able to absorb her feelings for her.

That amazing horse got her to trust and feel safe to talk to us about it. And all of this happened in under an hour! After she shared her pain with Dodger, she gave him an apple cookie. Then we went inside to my office, and I let her continue to vent and talk and be angry. When her mother arrived to pick her up, Katie's countenance was lighter, and I could tell she felt a bit more empowered. I give all the credit for that to Dodger. He had done his job beautifully and I stood in awe of his magic.

I continued working with Katie and even her younger sister Clarice. As an Empath, I can feel their frustration and sadness. We continued working with Dodger and the conversations with Katie and Clarice just kept getting better. For three months I saw them once a week and by the end of those 90 days, both girls were very clear that the problem with Daddy, was not their fault. It was his choices to drink and act like that. Daddy did finally go to rehab and got himself a small townhouse to live in. The girls were excited and were ready to forgive him and with a clean slate, start a healthy relationship with him.

It worked for about two weekends until their Mom had to go pick them up in the middle of the night again. He had relapsed and again the girls were alone and on their own while he was passed out. I did a short tune up with them and they were still clear it was his choice and had nothing to do with them. Currently, they see him in short, supervised dinner visits and where many circumstances like this can lead a child to never dream of a healthy life plan for herself, Katie now reports she wants to be an artist, learn French and study music!

As long as she believes she can do it then I am thrilled that Dodger and I gave her the wings to soar into a dream for herself!!

As I have heard so many times and said so many times, "How people treat you is their karma, how you respond, is yours"- Wayne Dyer

On a side note, her mother is getting married again to a nice, loving man.

He is supportive of Katie and Clarice and they love him and trust him.

Even when we don't have a Present loving father in our lives, a good male role model can help so much. I explained to Sam, their new stepdad, that a Father plants the seeds in the garden, but the Daddy waters them and helps them grow.

When our father cannot do both, then at least to have someone loving and kind to tend to the soil and water us, we can grow to reach our full potential.

I was also asked to officiate the wedding! I love it when clients get married or even re-married and they ask me to officiate it. It's always a happy ending for sure!

Dodger working with one of my young coaching clients 2019.

Fear

"I learned that courage was not the absence of fear, but the triumph over it. The brave man is not he who does not feel afraid, but he who conquers that fear."—Nelson Mandela

Dodger certainly had a great deal of fear to work through and overcome. But he's not alone. Humans have the same kinds of obstacles to get past.

Rodeo cowboys and other equestrians suffer a fear called "the dreads," which happens after being thrown by a steer, bronco, or your own horse. It can paralyze you and create such fear that you never get on to ride again unless you face it and get back in that saddle right after the incident happens.

Unfortunately, I know firsthand what the dreads can do to you. About twenty years ago, I was working with an abused and neglected thoroughbred mare at the SPCA, the same place from which I had adopted Dodger.

I had decided to ride this mare and work with her to try to overcome her fears and mistrust of humans. She was a gorgeous brown bay color with black legs, but she had become very barn sour on top of her mistrust of people. Barn sour is what you call it when horses don't want to do any work and every time you ride them, they cannot wait to get back to the barn to eat or be with their buddies. By the way, the worst thing you can do in this case is let them run back to the barn, as they will try to fully gallop back and consequently knock you off.

But back to my story, I had tacked up this mare and decided to ride out in the arena and then do some riding in the back pasture area. The ride was going fine and I thought we were having a good time when, suddenly, the horse reared up and the reins slipped out of my hands! I thought quickly and went to jump off her, but my pride, combined with the memories of my barrel racing days, said, **"hell no!"** and I stayed on her. As she came down on all four feet, I leaned forward to grab the reins, and as soon as I did...*Crash!*

Let me just say the accident was totally **my fault**! I own it. It happened when I was about twenty years younger than I am now and I was **not** a life coach. Believe me, I handled horses differently than I do today!

To this day, I cannot remember what happened and exactly how I fell off this horse. I do, however, remember floating over my body, looking down at myself on the ground. My friends, who were thankfully at the ranch, too, were calling my name and leaning over me. They told me the ambulance was on the way.

I floated over my body for what seemed quite a while. I then remember I felt the presence of my grandmother Ester, who had passed two months prior, beside me. Then I was unconscious again, and I only opened my eyes when I felt the firefighters lift me into the truck. My head bumped when they set me down.

I woke up again in the hospital with my friend, Roy, right next to me and my now ex-husband with my year-old baby son Antonio in his stroller asleep. Shortly thereafter, I threw up and was taken in for x-rays. I had to stay in the hospital for four days. I was miserable, but worse, I was now afraid to ride!

Somehow, I survived that accident. The doctors could not believe I had come out of it with no broken bones. I was alive, but I probably should have been killed. One of the guys at the ranch saw the accident, and he said it was terrible how hard I hit the solid ground.

Now we've all heard the old adage, "If you fall off a horse, you get right back on!" I, of course, never got that chance. I had been rushed to the hospital instead and had to recover.

It was several months before I got back in the saddle and even then, I did it with a great amount of caution, but I couldn't bring myself to canter the horse. Cantering a horse means getting it to go faster than a trot but slower than an all-out gallop.

I would make my horse walk and trot with some anxiety, but I was too terrified to ask him to canter. I tried, but even when I got to that gait, I felt the need to stop every two minutes.

This is devastating for a person that loves horses like I do. I never stopped loving them or wanting to be with them, but I was terrified of getting thrown again. This fear was unforeseen, especially coming from me. I used to barrel race at full gallops with one foot in my stirrup when the games called for a dismount. I had had no fear of riding like the wind, as fast as my horse could take us.

I never told anyone about my paralyzing fear. I couldn't even tell myself. I lied to myself for years about this fear of cantering.

When I first got Dodger, he bolted during our first ride. It freaked me out, so I jumped ship. I never tried to canter on his back after that. He would get his cantering in but in the round exercise pen.

Then I got my Quarter Horse Blue, who was a Reining horse. Reining is a form of competition riding in which the rider guides the horses through a precise pattern of circles, spins, and stops. He was used to zooming into a ring at full gallop and coming to a sliding stop and then spinning around and around and racing back out in the shortest time. I knew I couldn't canter him. I tried but stopped. I was terrified of what would happen if he took off and I fell off again.

It was horrible for me. I knew I had to overcome this fear of mine somehow. I kept envisioning accidents like those of actor Christopher Reeves and so many other equestrians whose falls from horses wound up with them paralyzed or worse, dead. I didn't want to be one of those people.

In the three years I have had Dodger and Blue, I have ridden, taken them on trails, worked them in the round pen and certainly used them for my coaching with clients. My horses have been phenomenal, but I owed them the canter.

I remember hearing that if you don't let your horse canter, they will become very frustrated and possibly get so antsy that it could make the situation worse. It's never a good idea to just let your horse stand in the pasture or the stall for long periods of time. They get bored, and it's not in their nature to be inactive.

My guys spend a lot of time in the pasture, so they weren't pent up, and that was on my side. I decided to take Blue and Dodger on a long trail ride one weekend with some friends. Dodger is so easy to ride now, I put my friend Jill on his back, and we have a great time on the trails. I figured if I got Blue tired, I could let him canter a bit, but he wouldn't push too hard to go full out. As we rode through the beautiful forest in North Georgia, the trees were green and full of singing birds. It wasn't too hot, but we had ridden about seven miles already. I decided to canter Blue.

As I made the kissing sound that directed him to pick up speed, he raised himself to a canter. As he did, he got so excited he began to buck. We were on a narrow trail path. I got nervous and reined him in. He tucked his head under with a shutter indicating he was pissed because I was holding him back. I knew it and it was my fault. I got him under control, and he walked nicely, but I felt so bad. I was a chicken, a terrible leader, and my horse had just lost a lot of respect for me.

After we arrived home, I rinsed them both off and fed them. I spent some extra time with Blue, just talking gently to him. I was hoping he would understand, but what was there to understand? I was afraid. And he knew I didn't trust him.

The very next day, I got up early and saddled him. I led him into the round pen and got on. He didn't stand still and kept moving. I took a deep breath and tried to connect with him in a gentle, calm way. I finally got on his back, and we began to walk. After a few minutes of trotting, I thought I would muster up my strength and try a canter.

I did, but again he tucked under and gave a little buck! I had him trot around the arena and do something at which I knew he wouldn't fail. I like to end my work out on a good note always. But we had no success with the canter. The next day I got up and did it all over again. I tried to get in the saddle, but again, he moved. I finally got him to stand still, rewarded him, and then started to walk on again. I got up my nerve to canter again, so I made the kissing sound again. But he wouldn't canter. It was as though he was saying, "Forget it, you are too scared. I give up."

So again, even though we didn't canter, I made sure we ended on a good note with something else. Then once again, the third day, back to it. He wanted to give up, but I just couldn't, and after seven days of work, Blue finally began to stand still for me to mount. But the canter was still not happening.

Two more weeks passed, some of the days called off due to rain. I knew I had to postpone in the name of safety, but the longer I waited the more I dreaded doing it.

Then finally, on July 5th, I had made up my mind. My husband Justin was at home. He is a retired paramedic, so I knew if something happened, I was in good hands. I asked him if he would help me with a horse project. He agreed although I knew he had no real experience with horses.

I saddled Blue and led him into the round pen where I attached a long rope to his halter. I left his halter on under his bridle to be able to attach the lunge line rope so that Justin could stand in the center of the arena holding the line while I rode Blue and attempted the canter again.

As we went around in the circle, I took some deep relaxing breaths and envisioned Blue and myself cantering with no bucking and really enjoying it. As I came around the corner in a trot, I told my husband to get ready for the canter. I leaned a little forward and "kissed," and Blue went into a canter as smooth as silk!

I felt safe after 20 seconds of no bucking, and I relaxed in the saddle. The connection between Blue and I was amazing! I could feel his joy at being able to canter with me on his back, and I am sure he felt my joy being able to trust him!

Blue and I cantered on and on around the pen as tears rolled down my face. I forgot how much I loved cantering! It was magical. I had faced my fear, and Blue and my husband had helped me. Justin had had no idea that I had this fear. I confessed it to him before we started and explained why this was so important for me to conquer. I guess I'd worn a poker face for so long, he was shocked to learn I had this fear.

For a moment, I stopped Blue. I hugged him and praised him. He could tell I was happy and he had done well. Then, once again, I leaned forward and kissed and we took off cantering again. I was flying! I was light as a feather, and it felt as if the earth was standing still. It was a moment that will come back to me one day as I review my life. I was happy! I loved cantering, and I could have done it all day long.

After about forty minutes of cantering, I got off Blue and thanked him. I hugged him and gave him a handful of treats that he gladly accepted.

That Sunday changed everything for him and me. He is mine and I am his, too, and we will fly again and again.

The experience changed my husband as well, and I believe we connected more, too! I invited him to help me to lunge a horse, which was something he had never done before. I showed him how to saddle and bridle a horse, and then I let him wash Dodger as I washed Blue. Justin said he had never connected with a horse like that before. He now knows how it feels. One day, I will teach him to fly, too, but for now, Blue and I have felt that magic, and it freed us both!

Fear is the one thing that, if given enough power, can take away our quality of life. Facing a fear is the best thing we can do to unblock the path to our joy, our love, our dreams, and our life's music.

Authenticity is All Important

"The more you work at just being yourself, the more likely you'll feel purposeful and significant in your life." -Wayne Dyer

It's not always easy to be honest about who we are or how we feel. It requires vulnerability and the risk of being hurt, rejected, or embarrassed. For a lot of us, that's not something we are willing or able to do. I understand. The world can be a scary place, full of misunderstandings, judgments, and outright abuses. These types of things have hurt most if not all of us, and it doesn't feel good. To protect ourselves from potential pain, discomfort, and humiliation, we can wear different "masks."

We may be one person at home, another person at work, another with friends—or we may have masks we wear only when interacting with specific individuals. These masks can help us feel safe and accepted or give us a sense of confidence. And we may not realize we are wearing them because we've done it for so long. The sad thing is we can go through daily life and never truly be ourselves. But what would happen if, instead of hiding behind our masks, we learned to develop genuine strength and confidence and no longer needed them? Horses can help you with that.

How on earth do they do that? It's simple. Horses can spot a fake. Humans can act calm on the outside, but horses can see any chaos that's churning on the inside of us. They can see it because there is no duality in nature; in nature, what you see is what you get.

If a horse is frightened, it doesn't care what you think about that. They don't pretend to not be scared. Only humans do that. If a horse is in pain, they don't act like they are fine. Only humans do that. You get the idea. Horses will always spot the human who is suppressing their true feelings. Horses don't care *why* you aren't being honest; they just know you aren't, and they will call it out—if you're paying attention to their cues.

As an equine specialist who works in equine-assisted sessions with therapists and clients, I regularly witness firsthand what happens when a client isn't being honest with himself or herself. The scenario typically goes that the therapist will ask a client how they were doing that day and the client says, "I'm fine." But if they aren't indeed "fine," the horse's behavior will show it has detected the falsehood. Depending on the horse, he or she will avoid the client, get agitated, get nippy, or be pushy toward the client, the therapist, even me! That is always a red flag that the client isn't being honest about their feelings—or maybe they aren't aware of how they really feel.

It's important to note that humans are complex creatures, and our brains can compartmentalize and suppress emotions to help us cope. That said, we may not always be aware that something is bothering us. This is especially true of those who suffered trauma and those who learned from their caregivers that they aren't allowed to have their own feelings. Have you ever had a situation change for the better and you felt enormous relief and then stopped and thought, "Wow, I didn't realize that was bothering me as much as it was!" It's exactly like that. Sometimes we just don't realize it.

The good news is that the horse will know what's going on inside of you. This explains why working with horses in equine-assisted activities helps speed up the process of resolving suppressed emotions and healing trauma. Sometimes, absolute honesty seems almost a foreign concept to the clients with whom the horses and I work. I have seen my horse call out a client on the spot. It can manifest in very subtle behavior like the horse's refusing to walk with them or clear behavior like stopping dead and turning their head in the complete other direction away from the client. The horse will not even look at the client until the client comes clean with their truth.

However, when the client starts to be open, the horse's behavior immediately changes for the better. The horse begins to relax, and the negative behaviors stop as the horse's protective instinct returns to a normal baseline. This happens because the pent-up, frenetic energy inside the client has been allowed to get some release. This is when real life change begins for the client. They are now able to receive the tools and insight they need to heal as their confidence builds and their masks begin to slip away.

Against the Wall

"Raise your words, not your voice. It is rain that grows flowers, not thunder."—Rumi

In my role as an equine specialist, I've come to understand it's the simple things that create the deepest respect between horse and human. Your mood when you enter the barn is paramount. You day to day interaction with your horse establishes your relationship. Going many days without visiting can degrade that relationship. It was because of the deep bond I had with this group of therapy horses that I found myself and two other humans in a situation I can only call divinely inspired.

Looking back on this story, I believe the horses knew what they wanted to happen in that session minutes before we entered the arena. I had met the therapist and client in the entryway leading to the new arena. We'd exchanged pleasantries, and I was preoccupied with our conversation as I opened the arena door.

Snort! The herd leader stuck his head through the opening and snorted again. I motioned and voiced a request to him to back up now. He snorted again. It's not safe to have a horse dart through a door and over you, right? Horses are far more powerful than humans, and it's an important part of my job that I maintain everyone's safety.

"Back," I requested again, but instead of the lead horse moving away, two other horses lined up next to him.

Trust! It felt as though that word hit me in the chest. I closed the door a bit and asked the therapist and her client if they trusted the horses and me. They said yes. So, we proceeded. The horses were in the doorway of the arena, and the therapist, client and I slipped to the left. Our bodies pressed against the wall and slid slowly, quietly into the arena until the three of us were completely inside.

The client was closest to the door, so she shut it. Now this is where it gets interesting. The three of us were shoulder-to-shoulder against the wall. In front of each of us was a horse. Tango was in front of me, Magic was in front of the therapist, and Galleon was in front of the client. When I say, "in front of us," I mean their noses were literally several inches from our chests. The horses simply stood there. They were still, no movement. They showed no aggression, only determination to be understood.

Sometimes in sessions you have to just let things happen. This was one of those times. Several minutes passed and the six of us hadn't changed position. I remember thinking it was odd the therapist was allowing this though I was glad of it.

The next thought that popped unbidden in my mind was the word suicide. Bang! Tango pushed his nose into my chest and then slightly to my right, in the direction of the client. Holy cow! Did he hear me? I thought the word suicide again. Bang! Again, he pushed his nose into my chest and then toward the client.

I remember thinking, let's be scientific about this. I'm going to repeat the thought again. For the third time, I thought the word suicide and again, Bang! Tango banged his nose into my chest and toward the client. A shiver ran down my spine—the kind of shiver you get when in the presence of the Divine.

So I asked the client, "Have you or has anyone you know attempted suicide?"
 Immediately she spoke, "My boyfriend committed suicide six months ago." The therapist and the client began talking in hushed tones.

The three horses, all in unison, turned and walked away from the three of us. I was standing against the wall of the arena alongside the therapist and the client. I felt a sense of astonishment. Did that really happen? I could hear the therapist and the client talking until their conversation drifted off and stopped. There was another pause. No talking. Silence. I was standing against the wall asking myself over and over, "Did Tango really read my thoughts? Or did I read his?"

Lost in my reverie, I hadn't noticed it, but the horses had lined up in front of us again, the same horse as before in front of each of us. There was silence as we realized that, yes, that did just happen, and it was about to happen again.

I thought to myself: What is this woman's struggle? Once again, Tango pushed his nose into my chest and then toward the client. I asked the question aloud, and the therapist and client  broke the silence once again and talked together. Again, the horses left us standing against the wall. At that point, I was dumbfounded.

As all of this was happening, I remember feeling a kind of numb sensation through my body. My mind was racing and there was a pulling sensation in my chest. I can't explain it any better than that; it was a pulling in my chest that was connected to the three horses in that arena.

This situation happened a third time, and I suddenly remembered hearing that several therapists and coaches knew Galleon—the horse that had positioned himself in front of the client—had a reputation for seeking out clients who'd lost people to suicide or had attempted suicide themselves. He would home in on any client who was having suicidal thoughts every single time!

Finally, when we had determined the session was over and as the three of us humans slid to the right along the wall and out of the arena door, the connection I had with the horses was broken. The numbness and the pulling in my chest were gone, but I was left with a racing mind.

I had so many questions. Can this be repeated? Can all the horses do that? Can I have this connection with a horse at will? I wanted to grab the first person that would stand still and let me tell her what happened. This was a pivotal time for me. This was when I truly accepted that the Divine was working through these horses. I was to listen and learn from them, and so I did.

Later, at the end of that night, I was so excited I couldn't wait to process this experience with the therapist. I walked into the therapist's office and expected to share our mutual astonishment about what had transpired today with the three horses and the client. But I was totally disappointed and dumbfounded that she'd had no idea what had happened. She had missed the whole amazing experience!

Teaghlach: Celtic for Family

"Before the inside of a horse can be right, the inside of the person needs to be right." —Tom Dorrance

Sandra was a single, high-powered executive in her mid-forties who lived in Michigan. She was going to be in Atlanta for work and asked if she could meet with me over the weekend. She arrived at my farm on Friday afternoon and as she approached the barn, my horses picked up their heads and looked at her.

I was happy to meet her but, as Sandra walked toward me, I could tell through her body language that she struggled with a lack of confidence and was sad and lonely. Dodger approached her and Sandra, who loves horses, reached out to pet him. I knew Dodger had already been able to see even more about Sandra than I could.

After she said hello to the horses, she and I sat down and talked. Sandra was well educated and very professional, but I perceived that her sense of power was based on pleasing her employers, not on what she brought to the table. While she was able to do her job well, she felt intimidated and bullied by one of her male bosses.

She was most likely smarter than he was and probably better at her job, but she still felt invisible and small in his presence. As brilliant as she was, she had no voice and was tired of feeling this way. The question was *why* did she feel this way? What had created this powerless image of herself?

I began asking questions. Did she feel this way with everyone or was it just this boss? Did he have a reputation of being controlling and abusive with everyone, or did he only act this way with her? She told me it didn't seem that her boss acted like this with everyone, just her. And she had no other issues with other people in the office. Why did she have these issues with him?

Then I asked her what the relationship with her father was like. She said it had been good, or at least okay, when she was growing up, but she had a big brother who used to bully her horribly. And in that moment, we discovered the root of her problem.

Sandra's older brother had been very rough on her when she was a child. He pushed her, shoved her, and was a constant threat to her during her entire childhood. I followed up with a question that completed the puzzle: was she intimidated around female bosses or just the male ones? She thought about it a moment and as the light came on, the answer bolted out of her mouth. "It was only the men!" That is exactly what I expected her to say.

We had been able to identify the root of her issue with her boss quickly. Now I knew the work that had to be done to heal the root, and Dodger was the key to that. I explained to Sandra what I felt was wrong and once she heard it out loud, she agreed and got excited, asking if she could be fixed. I laughed and told her I was sure we could help her feel a lot better. We agreed she would come back the next morning and begin our work.

The next morning, Sandra arrived, excited and nervous to get started. I reassured her it was all going to be fine and encouraged her to lean into the process. I would need one hundred percent effort and acceptance on her part to help her in this transformation, especially since we had only a limited time to work together.

My hope was this would be the last Saturday Sandra would feel afraid of men in this way. When traumatic things happen in our lives, we can still react to them in the present as if they are still happening. This is what was happening with Sandra with her boss, based on the experience she had endured from her brother. She perceived every man in authority as a bully and shrank around them.

We agreed to do the letting go exercise, which is an exercise I often use to help purge pain and anger from someone's body. As I blindfolded a seated Sandra and gave her a pillow, I helped her relax enough so she could go back to the first memory she had of her brother bullying her. She was able to let herself remember, which is a difficult but courageous thing to do, and she beat that pillow to a pulp and, in the safe space of my farm, yelled out if she was yelling at her brother and told him how what he had done had hurt her.

The letting go exercise is a fantastic tool for helping clients release stored pain and anger. I had seen this exercise used in different forms and, while I believe they all work, I'm partial to this one. One other technique I love to use is a beating on a punching bag. Adding motion to emotion helps release all the pent-up feelings we hold inside of us. I guide clients in the process of releasing and clearing out their "inner closet."

Imagine you have a closet within you that is jammed with all kinds of garbage, and it's so full, you cannot even open the door. When we remove the garbage inside, we have room for good things—new memories, more love, and greater joy!

After Sandra released the anger and pain caused by her brother, I switch her to claiming her life and who she is to her brother. It's the same exercise, only now I guided her to loudly state who she is—that she is strong and NOT invisible!

When she was done, Sandra was exhausted. She sat quietly breathing, tears having soaked the bandana used to cover her eyes, and her hands firmly held the pillow. She had released the negative emotions, reset her core beliefs about herself, and now we could begin the healing.

I always give my clients the choice to forgive the ones in their life who have hurt them or not. It's entirely up to them, and I don't judge their decision either way. But I do emphasize that, by forgiving, we are not condoning what that person did to us, we are merely releasing them and allowing ourselves the freedom to not carry that burden any longer. When I asked Sandra if she wanted to forgive her brother, she immediately said yes in a confident tone.

This moment for me is so beautiful. As an empath, I feel the emotions, pain, and sadness of my clients. When they release it, I can literally feel the clearing inside myself, like the weight being removed. At the end of these exercises, I offer plenty of hugs and praise. It is hard to do this work, and I am proud of my clients and thankful they have trusted me to guide them into the core of their pain and back out again.

This releasing work usually takes a few hours and I always let the client know to plan on being completely exhausted afterward. Sandra and I took a break. I provided her with lunch and had her drink a lot of water. We sat outdoors under my two-hundred-year-old oak trees and enjoyed the sound of the wind blowing and the birds singing. Just sitting quietly in nature can be rejuvenating to our souls. Mother Nature is so generous.

After Sandra had eaten lunch and rested for a bit, we started to work with the horses. Dodger was waiting and watching everything from the pasture. I handed Sandra his lead rope to go get him and walk him into the round pen. The purpose of this exercise was to help Sandra learn how to be a leader and work with someone. I explained to Sandra about the herd, just like I have many times to other clients. Sandra now needed to learn how a new way of communicating in a way that exuded power, not fear or shame.

As Sandra gently pet Dodger, I explained how; by getting Dodger's feet moving and her telling him what to do in a gentle but firm way, that Dodger will trust that she is a good leader and will do as she asks. But she needs prove it to him first.

In the round pen, I showed her how to "send" a horse in the direction she wanted him to go simply through body language. She caught on quickly and had the 1,000-pound animal at her command. Sandra could hardly believe how empowered she felt. I could see her face break into a huge smile as newfound confidence radiated through her.

I asked her how this felt compared to how she felt a few hours ago. She told me her past felt like a lifetime ago and she felt much lighter and stronger—like she could be a leader in her office and gain her boss's respect now. Dodger came into the center with her and looked at her eye to eye, as if to ask, what's next? He was standing about two feet away from her out of respect, not standing in her zone or being pushy. Soon, she had gained the respect of this most noble of creatures.

I ask Sandra to drop the lead rope and invite Dodger to come closer. He took a moment and finally stepped forward. I asked her what she wanted him to do. She replied that he needed to keep walking towards her. I told her "No, you need to take a step towards him and show him that you are a team and that you are willing to not only compromise but work together. He is showing you good faith; you must show him the same good faith and respect."

That step towards Dodger was huge for Sandra. She was moving in strength toward her new life. Once she took that step towards Dodger, I asked her to hug him. It took her a minute, but she put her arms around his neck.

Dodger lowered his head down to over her heart chakra and after a minute went by, the floodgates of her heart opened again, and she began to cry. Dodger stood there, taking in all that beautiful, released energy. He was her rock and she had a safe place to cry and be loved.

This had all happened in one day. It was successful day. I stood with tears in my eyes watching this all unfold before me. Dodger and I had partnered together to help this hurting woman, and I was once again reminded why he and I do this work.

As we finished up, I asked her to lead Dodger into the barn and give him a treat. She opened her hand flat with the tiny apple cookie in her hand and as he took it gently, he pushed her with his head in a playful way and she laughed.

She thanked Dodger and me and drove back to her hotel room to rest. I suggested she spend time on Sunday doing something nice for herself. We agreed to continue with online sessions when she returned home.

She called me when she returned home and told me she had spoken to her brother. For the first time, she had the courage to tell him how much he had hurt her and how it had affected her life. He apologized and they cried together and were able to start healing their relationship, just in time. Three months later, her brother was diagnosed with cancer.

As devastated as Sandra was, she became his rock and was there for him as he passed. Sandra is so grateful that she had forgiven him and had been able to have the close, loving relationship with him she wanted but had always been afraid to ask for.

We often don't realize that the challenges we go through are there to build us from the inside out and guide us into becoming who we are meant to be. Sandra now has an even closer relationship with her father and has since created her own practice as an equine-assisted life coach! Sandra now has ten beautiful acres in Michigan and has adopted five horses – once a client, now a coach. Before she and I met, Sandra had no idea she was meant to be a healer. But Dodger and I knew.

Tug of War

"There are two horses inside the human mind—the horse of good and the horse of evil. Each horse pulls the human towards their own inclinations. If the horse of evil is fed, then evil reigns over the mind, whereas if the horse of good is fed, then goodness prevails."—Abhijit Naskar, Aşkanjali: The Sufi Sermon

I had been an equine specialist for a while when this next story took place. I met the therapist, Kate, and her client outside the new arena. This particular client wasn't easy for me to work with for a specific reason. She had a lot of negative energy surrounding her. It wasn't the typical negative energy that some of the clients had due to their traumatic history; rather it was much deeper, as if something were attached to her. I always felt uncomfortable in her presence.

As an equine specialist, I believe in being professional at all times; both in and out of the session. I put aside my personal feelings of discomfort and did my job to the best of my ability for the client. I'll call the client, "Storm", comparable to the client's choice of name.

Storm had worked with a particular horse for most of her time at the facility. She normally worked with Tango. He was a big, beautiful Belgian paint cross and almost everyone who saw him fell in love with him, me included. Tango was the leader of the seven-horse herd.

As I grew into my role as equine specialist, I found it useful not to know too much about a client's history because I felt it interfered with my observations of what transpired between horse and client. Lacking those details, I could see the two interact as beings instead of as a horse and a "diagnosis."

The three of us, Storm, Kate, and I walked into the new arena to join Tango, the two women ahead of me. It was late in the day on a warm summer afternoon, and the sun cast long shadows into the arena. I closed the door behind us, and as I looked down to take another step, I saw Storm's shadow stretch out behind her.

I pulled my foot back in a kind of jerking motion before it hit the arena sand. The shadow cast from Storm looked like it would be sticky like tar if I touched it. And the shadow made me feel like it would be difficult to shake off its residue should I touch it.

So, there we were, Kate and Storm walking ahead with me trying not to step into Storm's shadow as we made our way into the dry lot looking for Tango.

I must have looked odd because Kate turned around and asked what I was doing. I didn't answer. How could I? What would I say?

I had the halter and lead rope already with me to catch Tango. Tango was always difficult to catch, but I had a trick I would use with him if I needed it. Kate asked Storm if she wanted to catch Tango herself, and she said no.
So, I proceeded like I would any other day. I repositioned the halter and lead rope to my right hand. Kate and Storm were talking in the background. Normally, I could catch Tango in a few minutes, but he was not having any of it. I

checked myself – how was my energy? Was I throwing him off?

Then I noticed it. Tango was dodging Storm's shadow, too. He would move around Kate and jump over Storm's shadow trying to avoid it if possible. Oh, man, Tango must have felt the negative energy, too. I felt bad for him because it was my job to catch him and bring him to that negative energy. What should I do?

To help Tango out, I moved farther away from Kate and Storm. Tango settled down a bit. I used my trick to catch him. I approached on an angle, not a straight line. I turned my energy source, my chest, away from him and allowed him to come close to me and then I laid the lead rope across his back. He took a few steps and then stopped, I quickly haltered him, reassured him that I had his back, and that I would be with him the whole time.

As Tango and I got closer to the client, his energy changed. His head got high, his nostrils flared, and his ever-expressive eyes rolled slightly back in his head. It hurt me to see him like that. He began to fight the lead rope.

Before Tango and I got any closer to Kate and Storm, I had Tango's back and suggested we try another horse. Kate asked her and Storm said she didn't mind if we tried working with another horse.

I released Tango, and he lurched away from me as quickly as he could. He covered a lot of ground in a few short steps. I felt relieved for him, but now I had to bring another horse into the situation.

Caesar was close, so I haltered him. Kate laughed and said, "How can you put Tango's huge halter on little Caesar?" There wasn't time left in the session to get Caesar's halter, and I would make Tango's halter fit Caesar, and that's what I did. I simply tied and tucked the leftover end inside the halter, it wasn't perfect, but for the few minutes that remained in the session it would do.

As I began to lead Caesar to Kate and Storm, out of nowhere Tango nervously trotted up alongside to Caesar. He got himself between Caesar and Storm. The closer Caesar and I got to Kate and Storm the stiffer Caesar's walk became, and Tango was wide eyed.

I unsnapped the lead rope from Caesar and stepped away. Tango immediately grabbed his halter in his teeth. He kept doing this, and each time he got a hold of the halter, he pulled in the opposite direction from Kate and Storm. Caesar dug his hooves into the dirt, Tango pulled at the halter, and I felt sick.

After about the third pull, Caesar seemed to figure out what Tango wanted and the two walked hurriedly away from where Kate and Storm were standing. Tango still had the halter in his mouth.

Kate and Storm laughed and remarked how cute it was that Tango and Caesar were playing. I felt a squeezing in my chest; I literally felt pain. Oh my God, Tango wasn't playing. He was trying to get Caesar away from the negative energy-surrounding storm.

I remember hearing Kate say the session was over and thanked me for my help. I could hear their voices trailing off as they laughed at Tango and Caesar's "playing" and said what a fun session it turned out to be.

I stood there next to those two horses and cried. Tango wouldn't let go of Caesar. I undid the halter from Caesar's little head, and it flopped down, dangling from Tango's mouth. It took me several minutes of petting those horses and reassuring them that everything would be all right.

Caesar was the first to release the negative energy with my help; he wheeled around, bucked out, and joined the other horses. Tango stood there longer. I told him I was sorry he had to experience that negative energy. He lowered his head and turned toward the other horses. I told him he was all right. He looked and pushed his huge head against my cheek and walked away. I looked at the ground and watched the long shadow of Tango meet up with and mix with the rest of the herd.

The Deepest Wounds Need the Deepest Healings

"There are things that the horse did for me that a human couldn't."—Buck Brannaman

Childhood is a rough time for many people. When it should be wonderful and full of awe, sometimes it is full of sad memories and pain. As children, we are subjected to what our parents do—whether it is alcoholism, drugs, abandonment, or neglect—and it can affect us in the subtlest of ways. Sometimes the parenting wasn't bad; per se, something like a dutiful parent having to work multiple jobs while being away from their family.

And those effects follow us into adulthood. One of my clients came to see me when he was almost sixty years old. Jason was a retired firefighter and truly was a hero. He'd earned many commendations and accolades for his service, yet he was suffering. When it came time for him to retire, he was miserable and had lost his edge and his passion.

He had lived a great life but suffered with angry outbursts when things didn't go the way he thought they should go. I immediately sensed control issues with him and asked about his childhood.

He was very reluctant to talk about his parents. He said only that he loved his parents and had wonderful memories with them. I suggested we sit outside on my beautiful four acres that was shaded by several two-hundred-year-old trees. I brought the horses out to graze and meet Jason.

Blue walked up to him and then continued walking off to find some grass. Dodger, however, walked up to Jason and began rubbing all over him. Not because his head was itchy but because he was sensing Jason needed some love and a friend. Jason wasn't sure how to react to Dodger, but I suggested that he just stand and let Dodger love all over him. Jason began laughing, and he and Dodger became friends.

Dodger then walked off to graze beside Blue. The two horses walked over the small hill on my property that leads to a wild garden they enjoy that you cannot see from where we were sitting.

Jason and I began talking and after about twenty minutes, he became relaxed and more comfortable. He told me his father had built their house on several acres and how cool it was that his father and mother had worked so hard to build the house. But they never finished it; and worse, left several old, rusted, broken cars and trucks sitting in the yard that took up most of property.

Jason admitted he had been terribly embarrassed by this as young boy. Several of his friends' parents never allowed them to come over and play because the property and the house were such a mess.

He had tried to help his dad get more organized, but it never worked. His dad became resistant and angry. Jason was so frustrated with the yard and the unfinished house that one day, at the age of fourteen, he took a hammer and nails and tried finishing the house himself. He was not successful.

He reported that many times and many of his own houses later, he just couldn't seem to finish projects. Walls were left unpainted, and room construction was never concluded. In trying to complete these projects, he was so disorganized that he lost tools all the time and was still trying to use his father's old, decrepit tools.

Oftentimes, the tools would break and he would try to fix them, but if he couldn't, he would get angry and lash out at everyone. He punched walls and yelled, and his words were mean and ugly. Jason was lost.

After he told me about the house, he reported that his parents had been farmers and raised dairy cattle. Although it was generally a great life for a kid to be a part of, he was taught to take baths just once a week. He never learned to use deodorant until someone handed him some on the school bus one day. Jason had no idea what he was doing wrong and his self-esteem had suffered.

As an adult, he seemed passive-aggressive about his work, and his frustration, disorganization, and inability to finish anything had made him seem like an angry man that pushed people away. I knew Dodger and I could help him.

My first suggestion was to ask him to write his parents an impact letter.

The impact letter is a great way to write to someone in your life that had a huge impact on you in either a good or bad way. Jason's parents had passed on, but it was still important for Jason to write them the letter and read it aloud.

As he began writing, I walked away and sat in my big tree swing. As I looked out past Jason, I saw Dodger had come over the hill and was standing under a big tree about 200 feet away. The look on his face was priceless. I knew he was very connected to Jason and me on this day, and I felt he was asking me if it was time yet?

I smiled at him and told him out loud, "Not yet, buddy, but very soon." He turned around and walked back over the hill to Blue. Jason continued writing the letter. He had noticed this and was amazed that Dodger had taken such an interest in him.

After Jason was finished with the letter, I asked him to stand up and read it. Dodger just knew he was needed and came right over to Jason and stood beside him while he read the impact letter out loud. Jason began to cry. There was a lot of pain stored up inside of him for many years, and this was probably the first time he had allowed it to come out.

Jason decided to re-read the letter. This time, he sobbed. He sobbed at every sentence. After he finished, I asked him to sit with all those feelings for a little while. He sat processing everything. It all made sense.

Jason would get so angry at not finishing a project or even his own home because his childhood home was never finished. His frustration only reminded him of his own father's "get to it when I can" attitude. His father worked a full-time job and traveled for business, so the house never really got done.

After several minutes passed, Jason said, "Okay, I'm ready." Then we got up and burned the letter. It burned quickly. He was obviously ready to let all of this go. We took a short break, and I put the halter on Dodger. Dodger by this time was waiting for us in barn. This horse just amazes me!

Jason led him into the round pen. I instructed him to begin walking in a circle with Dodger. Jason did and seemed a bit more relaxed and lighter. I asked him stop Dodger a few times and tell him his darkest secret, his scariest moment. Dodger remained calm and interested, tilting his ear towards Jason and being an attentive listener.

Then I asked Jason to tell Dodger what he feels he needs and wants most in his life. He whispered in Dodger's ear and, in an instant, Dodger backed away from Jason and turned his head away.

Jason was confused about what had just happened. I told him that Dodger was calling him out on his truth. I asked what the question was, and Jason said,

"I told Dodger that I needed to be happy, that I want to be happy."

I asked Jason to think about that for a few minutes. Dodger thinks you need something else. Then, Jason's eyes began to water, and he lowered his head.

"I need to be more grateful. I don't think I really appreciate all the blessings in my life." As soon as Jason said that, Dodger turned his head back to look Jason in the eye. Now Jason was crying. He understood, and it was Dodger that helped him get it.

Even though Jason had had a difficult childhood, he'd had two parents that loved him, a great career, a loving wife, and a family that appreciated him. That was all it took to help reset Jason: confronting his parents in a loving letter about his childhood and a horse named Dodger to open his eyes and heart.

Jason left that day walking lighter. He had a smile on his face and a glow about him.

I am happy to report, he is doing very well these days. He meditates in various ways to help him get quiet. I also taught him how to do a self–guided shamanic journey wherein he met his two spirit animals: the hawk and the white leopard.

He now reports feeling empowered and free. He's found his passion once again. He said he's going to pick up photography again, which was a hobby he'd greatly enjoyed in the past but had let languish there, and to start growing vegetables and herbs.

Jason had made peace with his past, which was necessary for him to move forward as his healthiest self.

Addictions and the Horse

"It's more important that you know your weaknesses than your strengths."—Ray Hunt

A while ago, I began working with a client that had an opioid addiction. He was determined to quit his drug habit; he had a lot to lose. He had a baby son, a fiancé and a new family if he wanted it. His entire biological family had had various addiction problems.

There had been overdoses, suicides, and his own mother was his supplier. This young man, in his late twenties, needed to make a massive change in his life. So, he chose my horses and me to help him out.

I was brutally honest with him in the beginning. An addict must want to quit. I witnessed that firsthand with my own son. Being very firm with my client, I told him if he wasn't serious about quitting that he shouldn't waste my time. He was clear: quit or lose his son and fiancé and maybe his life.

So, we went to work.

Dan had worked with therapists in the past, and "One or two were okay," he said. Please note, I am *not* slamming therapists in this book! Great therapists are worth their weight in gold/chocolate/whatever is a precious commodity to you. What I love about being a coach, though, is that I get to rock the boat. We learn we are off balance when we are uncomfortable.

I believe that people that are on the wrong path and being destructive to themselves sometimes need to hear the truth in a tough-love kind of way. I am a big fan of tough love. I used it on my own son, and I use it on my clients that need it. I am not going to coddle them and tell them what they want to hear. This is work. I get inside of you. I crack you open. You have to let me!

It's shocking, I know. I use colorful metaphors, too, but it creates more attentive hearing and a shock to your soul when you hear the truth about yourself. I am telling you your reality, your truth, and it may piss you off or it may make you cry but either way, you need to hear it. After they hear it, trust me, I am firm but very loving and supportive. I have found that people appreciate someone who is not afraid to tell them the truth.

Our first session was to help him let go of his past and all the pain and anger that were feeding his addiction—to release and clear out all those limiting beliefs that got stuck inside of him as a child. I also reacquainted him with his inner child; the little Dan that he had ignored all these years. This is a beautiful and very spiritual process. Joy replaces pain and love replaces feelings of unworthiness.

As a rule, a lot of tears come out when we heal one's inner child, and I have had people tell me they can feel an angel or presence in the room with us. I have no doubt this is true. This process can take two to five hours. The client is usually emotionally exhausted afterward. After healing their inner children, I send clients home to drink lots of water and sleep.

When Dan showed up for our next session the following week, we were going to work with the horses. Horses are game changers. I have seen huge benefits in people with addiction issues. There is actual healing, and a conscious decision is made to change their lives after such an encounter.

I have seen prisoners find themselves, maybe for the first time ever, in working with wild mustangs. Drug addicts and alcoholics become humbled and respectful with a horse because they know a horse won't buy into their lies and manipulations.

I asked Dan to stand in the pasture where my horses were grazing. As I stood off to the side observing, waiting to see which horse would approach. Usually Dodger, who thinks he is the Welcome Wagon representative of the farm, walks up to everyone; says hello and hangs out with him or her. This time, he didn't. He approached my client, looked at him, and kept walking right past him.

Blue on the other hand; my very tall, sometimes intimidating, quarter horse walked toward Dan and stopped about three feet away. He stretched out his neck and got a sniff of my client and turned his head to look at me and walked off. Neither of them wanted anything to do with Dan. That was interesting to me.

So, I asked him, "Are you high?" He said no but that he had had a really bad day, and he was stressed out and nervous about being here. I think my horses felt duality within him. They may have also picked up on his stress and the lie of him being here but not yet one hundred percent sure he could do this. Either way, Blue was the only one that had approached him, so Blue was his horse.

In this session, I had planned on mostly utilizing the horses. The boys (as I refer to my horses) had their halters on and were ready to work. It had been raining for three days in a row, so working in the arena in soaking wet ground was not a good idea for my horses, but we could do something that didn't require my horses running in that slick mud.

I usually clean the horse's stalls every day, but today I purposely left Blue's stall dirty. Drug addicts and alcoholics only think about themselves while they are using. It's not their true nature, but it's what happens to the brain when it's constantly taken out of a state of sobriety and into a state of hallucinations, when it's given a false sense of power and ability. They will find any way to get their drugs and alcohol—lie, cheat, and manipulate those that love them because it's easy. In other words, it's all about them.

Today, I wanted Dan to begin learning how to do for someone else, including horses. I told him of the plan for our session, and he didn't quibble at all as he picked up the rake and began cleaning Blue's stall. I have always believed that spending time with the earth and the animals, getting dirty, and caring for something other than yourself is really healthy. It is also relaxing and teaches you to daydream and connect in a different way. It is also humbling to clean up after someone or an animal.

After the stall was clean, I asked him to lead Blue into the hallway and connect him to the post to be groomed. This did not go as smoothly as you would think. Blue was very skeptical and kept his distance from Dan.

I asked Dan what he thought was happening between him and the horse. He said he felt that Blue could see right through him. Blue wasn't making it easy for Dan to lead him into the hallway to groom. Blue turned his butt toward him, and that really got Dan's attention.

I asked what he thought Blue was trying to tell him. He felt that Blue was not buying his attempt to be friends, as if Blue didn't believe him. I asked again where this showed up in his life. He realized that he has done that to people himself. He has turned his back on people that love him and chosen drugs over true friends and family.

After about twenty minutes of Dan's being gentle and, I believe, trying to be honest with Blue, Dan finally got Blue to turn his head toward him and let himself be led to the post. Dan slowly began brushing. Blue stood still and allowed the grooming and after a while, he relaxed and enjoyed it.

I asked him to lead Blue out to the arena and walk him inside. Blue went along just fine, but I noticed a calmer mood to Dan. In this short time of grooming and trying to be friends with Blue, he had already begun to see his own truths and that this horse was going to hold him to them!

As my client worked with Blue in the arena, Blue was still not fully invested. He was still somewhat skeptical, not sure about this guy. I decided to teach Dan how to set boundaries in his life and to learn it the horse way. I explained about the herd and how the lead mare will ostracize a young rude colt and tell him to leave. The colt will stay close enough to see the herd, but he won't be invited back in until he shows respect and humbly asks to come back. If the mare agrees, he will be allowed to return.

This story impressed Dan. I asked him again, "Where does that story show up in your life?"
He immediately understood the lesson. It reminded him of his fiancé and son that will kick him out of their lives if he doesn't quit drugs. Then I taught him how the herd teaches boundaries.

Setting boundaries with a horse is different from setting boundaries with people. The horse is a herd animal; his cues are picked up from the body language of the herd mare of any other horse within the herd. Horses set boundaries with horses by pinning back their ears, lowering their heads and thrusting their heads forward or even pushing their noses toward the other horse to say step back.

Obviously, we can't pin our ears back or snake out our necks but, by wiggling the lead rope, the horse will step back out of your zone and back into his. This is asking a horse to respect you and establishes leadership. If the horse ignores you and walks back into your zone, you wiggle the lead rope a bit tougher and say, "Get back," and he should.

You are telling him to move by performing an action he will understand. I do not support the idea of bringing a client into the round pen with a bucket of feed and when the horse approaches the bucket of food, the therapist tells the client to yell at the horse. You will create an angry, mean horse and you will ruin him. He doesn't understand why he's being punished. My simple method works fine. The client learns, and the horse is neither traumatized nor pissed.

When working with horses and people, it is important that you understand the herd mentality and why horses do all the things they do. Horses have their own wisdom, and this is what heals the client in so many beautiful amazing and magical ways. I am grateful for my horses and what they teach me every day.

Dan Tangled Up in Blue

"The horse is a mirror to your soul. Sometimes you might like not like what you see. Sometimes you will."—Buck Brannaman

After Dan learned from Blue how to successfully set boundaries, he felt fairly sure he could do better at setting his own boundaries with his drug-using friends and his own mother.

We then proceeded to spend time with Blue, just walking with him on his lead line around the arena. I suggested Dan talk to Blue about his drug addiction, and every now and then, I asked him to stop and tell Blue something personal.

At one point, I asked him to stop walking and tell Blue what he loves most. He whispered in Blue's ear, "My son and my fiancé." Then I asked him to hug Blue. He did and then I saw the magic. Blue reached around and hugged my client and then extended his nose as if to give him a kiss and a supportive pat. I cannot tell you the energy my client and I both felt at that moment. It took my breath away.

The walk continued and they stopped again. I asked him to tell Blue what was more important to him, drugs or his family. Dan told Blue his family meant more, but Blue saw right through it. He turned his head away from Dan, and Blue's message came across loud and clear.

I asked Dan if he was being honest. He said, "drugs used to be more important to me, but I am learning my family is." Blue obviously picked up some hesitancy in that statement and turned away from him again. It slapped Dan in the face. Blue didn't believe him and let him know it!

We wrapped up the session with a blindfolded trust walk through the woods behind my house. Then we burned an impact letter to his mom. It was a long session, but I felt it was the right thing. I also showed him how to meditate, and we sat on the ground under a huge Magnolia tree in full bloom in my front yard pasture.

Before he left, Blue came out to the fence as if he knew Dan was leaving. He just stood there so tall and majestic. It was a powerful statement Blue made. It was as if to say, I am here for you, but I will hold you to higher truths. Dan left humbled by the whole experience, as did I.

Obviously, some of the sessions with people go pretty long, often up to a few hours, but I would rather continue if we were making progress. I hate hearing, "Well, time is up. See you next week." If I am getting somewhere and the client has time, we will continue until we get to a good stopping point. The horse needs a break, too, and I follow their cues as well.

After a session with someone that has had a traumatic background, my horses spend time yawning and releasing all that energy. They pick it all up from the client. People think they are sleepy. Nope, that is what they do; they pick up the client's energy and then they need to release it. After every session, they get a lot of grazing and play time. They also get a juicy apple and a big thank you from me.

Dan is still working on finding out who he is without drugs. It's a difficult journey for sure. He had one slip up while we worked together. He bought some opioids and then decided to toss them out the car window. I considered that a win! He has become a better father to his young son and is working hard to make a living and focus on being there for his family.

There is a lot of forgiveness that needs happen. His significant other has endured a lot of pain and disappointment—something quite common in families of addicts of any sort. We talked a lot about consequences and that, while we are free to make our own choices, we cannot choose the consequences.

I reminded him I am only a guide to help him find his path, the path of least resistance without drugs, the path that eventually will show him after being successfully sober over time, who he can be. Blue already knows. Dan hopes he won't let Blue down.

Blue in session with Dan. Dan is explaining to Blue what is the most important thing to him; drugs or family. Dan tells Blue his priority is family. Blue calls him out on his lie. Blue helps Dan realize that though he wants family to be most important, he is still battling with his addiction. Dan is grateful that Blue held him to his actual truth.

Standing in the Peace of a Horse

"You are not working on the horse, you are working on yourself."—Ray Hunt

There is a lot of magic when working with horses. People usually think that working with horses involves just riding them or going to horse shows. It doesn't. When horsemen and -women only have that vision, they never develop the kind of relationship with a horse that opens up a world of magic: Magic healing, magic moments, and magic lessons learned.

As equine-assisted life coaches, Debra Johnson and I have seen the magic every day in our work in partnering with these beautiful creatures. In this busy, uncertain world of ours, the question clients seem to ask most often is in essence; how they can learn to stand in their own skin and find peace.

I always suggest making the time to meditate and sit with Mother Nature. More specifically, I have come to learn so many beautiful lessons about standing in *my* own skin and finding *true* peace from my two horses, Dodger and Blue, I now suggest client's use their relationship to them or other horses as a means of directly connecting with Mother Nature.

One day back in the fall of 2018, Dodger and Blue transformed all I was once sure I knew about meditation and being still. Let me tell you about it... It had long been my practice to walk outside to my pasture and bring a book to read to my horses. I usually do this on days when I have few or no clients or it's raining. Dodger especially loves hearing my voice as I read out loud. Blue will listen as well, but Dodger gets closer and likes to touch the book with his nose. These are always peaceful moments, but never before had they turned into what I experienced on this day with them both.

It was partly cloudy and there was a gentle breeze blowing. At first, Dodger stood close by, as usual, listening to me read as Blue stood beside the fence. I was reading the Buck Brannaman book called *Faraway Horses*. It's one of my favorites! My son gave it to me as a Christmas gift.

As I read this or any other book to my horses, I get pictures in my mind of what I am reading. They see those pictures, too. As do all animals, they speak in pictures. I learned that from my friend Dusty, and he learned it from a Native American Indian that taught him about horses at the young age of twenty.

Dodger then went and stood underneath his favorite Magnolia tree to listen from there. I approached Blue with book in hand and began gently stroking his neck. As I stood beside this sixteen-and-a-half-hand, angelic, calm, thoughtful being; his eyes pierced my own. So deep was this moment as was our connection. As a matter of fact, I was positive our souls connected. I noticed how much I relaxed and felt my body slow down, as if to meld together with Blue's. I lost myself in those large eyes of his, and I didn't fight it. I just let it happen. I wanted to be where he was. I wanted him to teach me.

Before I knew it, I was no longer having a relaxing moment of reading to them, but instead I had taken a step into their world. Dodger and Blue were showing me what peace truly is. It is difficult but let me try to describe it as best I can. It was the deepest silence I had ever heard. I stood softly petting Blue on his neck and then on top of his mane, the way his mother did when he was a young colt. In this moment of complete calm and peace, I felt us together go deeper and deeper into this incredible place he goes for his peace. I was honored that I was invited to join him.

As we three stood within two feet of each other, I could feel not only Blue's amazing peace but Dodger's as well. It was one of the most profound moments of my life. I had no thoughts of time or place, but I could feel myself going deeper and deeper into their world, or their *dimension* for a more accurate word.

I was wrapped up in an overwhelming feeling of love, and it almost felt Godly. Tears ran down my cheeks. I felt their energy of love and acceptance for me. As I stood softly stroking Blue's cheek, I noticed his breathing getting softer and softer.

Dodger approached then and stood just two feet away from Blue and me. His eyes were also closing as I whispered to him. I closed my eyes, too, and I envisioned him and me in the shady part of the pasture, him lying down in the soft grass with his head on my lap as I slowly rubbed his long neck. How I envied them.

This magical moment will live in me forever. I will never forget that feeling of utter peace and love that I received from them today, and I will go to them every chance I can

and get more of that feeling. You could say I am hooked.

So now when my clients ask about finding peace and being comfortable in their own skin, even when the world is chaotic, I have taught them how to stand with my horses and allow themselves to be taken wherever Dodger and Blue lead them. It is everyone's own private journey when partnering with the horses, and I trust my two to take my clients exactly where they need to go.

The results have been amazing, and not only have my coaching clients experienced this peace firsthand from meditating with my horses but they subsequently are able to meditate on their own and find their own peace at any time or place of their choosing.

Debra's Thank You

I am blessed and give thanks to the horses...

The horses that were gentle, patient, kind, and loved the hugs and kisses I gave them. Thank you for sharing peace and joy with me. The horses that were Zen masters of enlightenment and wisdom, I am humbled that you saw fit to allow me into your realm and learn your ways.

That drove me nuts, challenged me, and made me want to pull my hair out. Thank you because you didn't give up on me. You made me take a long hard look at myself, and I am the better for it.

Thank you for allowing me to become a student of the horse. To my family, thank you for your love and support. Thank you for your patience and for allowing me to wander this path less taken. Thank you for trusting me that I would find my way. I'm sure it hasn't always been easy for you to understand my crazy dreams and ideas. I'm sure you worried about me and wondered if I would ever find my way. I have found both my way and my voice because of you.

To my friends, thank you for letting me ramble on about horses. You have the patience of the saints. To my friends who gave me great advice when I was troubled and unsure of my next move, who watched thunderstorms roll across the sky and listened to the rain hit the barn roof with me, who made me laugh so hard my sides hurt, who helped me train horses into the wee hours of the night, who showed me another way of working with horses, and who were willing accomplices of late-night practical jokes, I thank you.

To Pam Kachelmeier, had I never met you, I don't know where I would be on this journey with horses. You inspired me to listen to my awakening spirit and trust the Divine. You are a woman of many gifts and generous with your knowledge. You have been a compass for my soul. You are a soul sister and friend.

To Gina Martell, you are an amazing human being. You have a tremendous gift for healing troubled souls with a grace and ease that is reserved for the sages of old. You have a wisdom that is not of this time, but rather from an ancient, faraway place where streams ran through dark forests rich with flora and fauna. You "see the unseen and hear the unheard." Thank you for your friendship and guidance. You, too, are a soul sister.

P.S. thank God you said, "Yes" when I half-jokingly remarked: "We should write a book" because few people would ever say yes and mean it!

Gina's Thank You

As I sit in my barn looking at my horses, I wish I could find better words than "thank you" because those two little words cannot express what I feel. My heart is so full of joy and gratitude for my whole life and where it has led me to this point!

From my heart, I am so thankful for those who have always stood beside me and supported me. I am grateful for my amazing warrior children, Robert, Tali, and Antonio (who are adults now). Being a single mom was rough, but I learned so much from you guys; you are my inspiration and, collectively, my rock!

I am grateful to my Uncle Wilson who loved me unconditionally and never hung up or left without telling me he loved me.

I am grateful for my dearest lifelong friends: Sandy, who has always been there to encourage me; Becky and Michele, who walked a tough path with me through our difficult childhoods; Jill and Giuliana and other friends that laughed and cried with me and have been there through thick and thin.

I am grateful for my sister, Veronica, who always believes in me; my father, Arnie, who, despite our ups and downs, taught me about being the Rock of Gibraltar; and my "Avo" (grandmother in Portuguese), Esther, who passed down her intuitive gifts to me. I am also honored by my clients that have trusted me to guide them and believed in both my horses and me.

I am eternally grateful to Dusty, who helped me learn to reconnect with my favorite animal in the world; Pam Kachelmeier, my equine-assisted coaching teacher and her amazing Equine-Assisted Coaching Association (EACA) course; Penny, my colleague, business consultant, and CPA; Debra Johnson, my very talented and powerful soul sister; Roy Pressman and Laurie Wagoner from the SPCA in Miami, Florida, for their exhausting mission of rescuing horses and thus introducing me to my equine coaches Artful Dodger and Heza Hancock King (Blue).

I thank my quarter horse, Punk, who was my guardian and best friend; Regal Lady; and my first horse that started it all, my Black Beauty. I thank you for being there during the most difficult and challenging moments in my youth. You saved my life.

I am most thankful for my amazing equine coaches, Dodger and Blue, for teaching me every day about their world and what it means to have a true friendship with a horse. You are my brothers with four legs. I am also grateful to my husband, Justin (my firewalk captain), who supports me, believes in me, and has learned a lot from my Dodger and Blue, too, whether he planned on it or not.

Thank you to Cynthia Wilkins, who was helpful with her advice and input at the very beginning of this book; author Jenny Pavlovic for her great writing advice and guidance; and Sid Korpi, our amazing editor who really helped us put this book together.

My thanks, too, to my dog, Amber, and three cats: Nietcha, Einstein, and Layla, who variously sat on my lap and/or under my feet as I wrote this book.

I dedicate this book to my mom, Sandra Eileen Crofoot Rhodes, whom I love and miss; and my grandfather, Joseph Stafford Rhodes, whom I never knew. We shared a special love for and understanding of horses. Thank you, Grandpa.

Also, I'd like to dedicate this to all the horses in the world, the wild ones, the loved ones, the misunderstood, and abused ones. You are truly my Anam Caras (soul friends in Gaelic).

About the Authors

Virginia "Gina" E. Deleo Martell currently lives in Woodstock, Georgia but is planning to move back to her home state of Florida to further expand her Equine Coaching business in a warmer climate!

Gina is Mom to her horses, Dodger and Blue; her equine coaches and previously rescue horses who lived at the SPCA in Miami. Gina is certified as a professional life coach (CPC), a Neurolinguistic practitioner (NLP), and an equine assisted life and relationship coach (EAC). She is additionally a member of the Equine Assisted Life Coaching Association (EACA).

Her studies began after attending a Tony Robbins UPW seminar in 2010 and once certified as a life coach through the Life Coaching Institute of Orange County, an IFC course, and studying with her mentor and friend Dr. Dennis Neder, therapist and life coach, her additional certifications followed as she began her work with coaching clients. She began with Firefighters, cops and soon after began specializing in women and children with abusive backgrounds including dysfunctional childhoods, abusive marriage and relationships. This was an area of passionate healing due to her own childhood and alcoholic mother.

Gina's thirty-four years in radio as an on-air radio personality and voice over talent, helped her gain confidence in becoming a dynamic speaker and having great interaction and a personal connection with her public when requested for speaking engagements or on air/tv interviews.

Gina additionally added Spiritual Coach to her education. This was a special gift she had since childhood but closed it off. Later in life after becoming a life coach, Gina realized how beneficial this gift could be in her coaching and working with the horses, so she sought out spiritual masters and teachers to help to open it once again within herself and now she applies it when appropriate in helping clients learn to quiet their minds by learning to meditate and forgive.

Gina is also an Animal Communicator. She practices daily meditations and works closely with Gaia, ("Mother Nature") in her session work and daily life.

"People ask me how long I have been an equine assisted life coach and I tell them, either ten years or sixty years because in truth, my entire life has been about my horses and my own personal growth to put me on this path to be able to partner with horses to help people heal and find their own personal happiness" -- Gina

Debra Johnson resides in New London, Wisconsin and she is Mom to Jeffrey and Ebby and Eeyore. Debra is an Equine Specialist (ES) who cares for all aspects of the horse, feeding, watering, and training and assists the therapist in an equine session.

Debra began her work in 2010 as a volunteer for a non-profit mental health facility where they partnered with horses as part of the healing process. She then acquired her ES and worked with youth and teens with trauma history which includes suicidal ideation. She continues her work with the horses and those seeking help from healing with horses.

In 1999, Debra worked with kids as a substitute teach for 4-K to 12th grade in all subjects.

At the age of ten, Debra began studying martial arts. Debra also holds a Third Dan Black Belt in American martial arts. She was also a martial art fighting competitor and instructor. Olympic gold medalist, Arlene Limas referred at the Diamond Nations in Minnesota where Debra placed third. Through her studying of martial arts,

Debra learned about Chi/energy flow in preparation for brick and board breaking demonstrations.

Ironically, Martial arts were the foundation that prepared Debra in her work with horses. Chi or energy surrounds everything and knowing this, Debra learned to apply it with the horses. A few years ago, she attended several healing ceremonies with an Oneida native medicine man Dennis King aka "Rocky."

Debra has incorporated this healing and lessons from Rocky and other spiritual teachers in her life to help assist her in her work with the horses.

"You are always one decision away from a different life"- author unknown

Index

.

. I felt awe, 30

"

"regular" humans, 18

A

About the Authors, 177

Abraham Hicks, 13

addict, 149

Addictions and the Horse, 149

Against the Wall, 115

amazement, 29

angels, 33, 36

Angels and Horses and Bad Apples, 85

Animal Communicator, 179

Animals, 20

Anna Breyenbach, 17

anxious, 79

Atlanta, Georgia, 33

Authenticity is All Important, 111

B

be a great mom, 32

become more authentic, 87

Blue, iv, 15, 79, 80, 81, 82, 83, 84, 85, 86, 103, 104, 105, 106, 107, 108, 109, 110, 141, 144, 152, 153, 154, 155, 156, 159, 160, 161, 162, 163, 165, 166, 167, 168, 174, 175, 177

C

capable leader, 72

check my attitude, 55

client, 18, 53, 54, 55, 76, 85, 86, 112, 114, 115, 116, 117, 118, 119, 120, 121, 128, 132, 133, 134, 136, 149, 151, 152, 156, 157, 158, 159, 161, 165

clients, 85

coaches, 40, 47, 120, 164, 174, 175, 177

coaching clients, 10, 98, 169, 177

Coaching with Children: Katie and

Clarice, 91

communicate with, 18

complex creatures, 113

confidence building, 75

connection, 89

connection between Blue, 108

courage, 99

D

Dan Tangled Up in Blue, 159

Debra, i, ii, 7, 15, 16, 26, 50, 70, 164, 170, 174, 180, 181

Debra Johnson, i, ii, 15, 26, 164, 174, 180

Debra's Introduction. *See*

Debra's Thank You, 170
Dedications, iv
Dodger, Blue, Tango, Eeyore, Jeffrey, Punk, Black Beauty, Regal Lady, iv
Dodger, iv, 15, 58, 60, 61, 62, 63, 64, 65, 67, 68, 69, 70, 71, 73, 74, 75, 76, 77, 78, 79, 82, 83, 84, 92, 93, 94, 95, 96, 97, 98, 99, 103, 104, 105, 110, 122, 124, 128, 129, 130, 131, 132, 141, 144, 145, 146, 147, 152, 165, 166, 167, 168, 174, 175, 177

Dodger's Journey Back to Himself, 68
Dr. Dennis Neder, 13, 177
drug, 33, 36, 149, 159
drug addict, 33
Dusty, 74

E

Ego, 86
empath, 41, 127
equine specialist, 112
equine-assisted life coaching, 10
Everglades, 62

F

Fear, 99, 110

fifty, 37
Fire Team, 13
floating over my body, 101
forgive them, 31
four days, 37
friend, 13, 31, 37, 47, 48, 55, 58, 70, 78, 79, 81, 84, 88, 89, 101, 105, 141, 166, 171, 175, 177
friends, 11, 12, 33, 40, 50, 58, 64, 91, 101, 105, 111, 141, 142, 155, 159, 171, 173, 176
From the Heart of Horses— Listen and You'll Learn, 48

G

Gaia, 19
Gaia,, 179
Galleon, 116, 120
get in the saddle, 106
Gina's Introduction, 10
Gina's Thank You, 173
giving up, 36
God, 36, 38, 138, 172
God's hands, 36
grandmother Ester, 101
grandparent's farm, 7

H

He Knew I was coming, so He Waited— Dodger's Story, 58
herd leader, 116

herd of wild horses, 50

his joy, 108

horse, 8, 9, 10, 11, 12, 14, 19, 21, 22, 23, 24, 25, 29, 39, 40, 43, 44, 45, 46, 47, 48, 49, 50, 52, 53, 54, 55, 57, 58, 59, 60, 61, 62, 63, 64, 65, 66, 67, 68, 70, 71, 72, 74, 75, 76, 78, 79, 81, 83, 85, 86, 87, 88, 89, 95, 99, 100, 101, 102, 103, 104, 106, 107, 110, 112, 113, 114, 115, 116, 118, 120, 122, 129, 133, 134, 137, 140, 146, 147, 152, 153, 154, 155, 156, 157, 159, 161, 164, 170, 175, 180

horse's protective instinct, 114

Horses are sentient, 21

Horses don't care, 22

hospital, 101

how do you ride horses?", 8

huge rock, 35

Humans love words, 24

I

I loved cantering, 108

I relaxed in the saddle, 108

I was flying, 109

I wasn't giving up, 37

If We Could Talk to the Animals …Wait a Minute —We Can!, 17

If you fall off a horse, you get right back on!, 102

innate connection, 19

inner battle, 31

It should be obvious, 43

It's easy, 32

J

January in northeast Wisconsin, 26

journey was rough, 31

Juan, 80

July 5th, 107

K

karma, 97

Katie, 91, 92, 93, 95, 96, 97

L

leap of faith, 76

life coach, 10, 13, 31, 38, 39, 40, 41, 91, 101, 132, 177, 178, 179

life's music, 110

little black cat, 15

love myself, 36

loyal, 88

M

magic, iv, 10, 29, 30, 95, 110, 159, 164

Magic, 26

magical, 9, 16, 30, 93, 108, 158, 168

majestic moment, 30

masks, 111

meditated, 79

meditations, 179

miracles, 7

mostly women, 39

mutual love and understanding, 16

My children, 32

My decision, 34

my fault, 101

My grandfather, 12

my greatest hopes, 65

My mother, 11

My path, 38

My Winter Vision, 26

N

natural intuition and

desire to help others, 13

negative energy, 133, 136, 138, 139

noble, 88

O

opioid addiction, 149

outstretched hands, 29

P

Pam Kachelmeier, 14, 40, 171, 174

paralyzing fear, 103

part of this magic, 30

Penny, 78, 79, 174

permission, iii

phobias, 75

power, 18, 110, 122, 128, 154

prankster, 60

prey animals, 21

pride, 100

primal roots, 19

R

Rebecca, 91

red flag, 113

rehab, 63

re-parenting, 35

Respect the Ride, 43

rough childhood, 12

S

Sandra, 122, 124, 125, 126, 127, 128, 129, 130, 131, 132, 176

Sandra's older brother, 124

Save the Horses, 44

shoulder-to-shoulder, 116

simple beauty, 28

simple things, 115

Skeptics, 17

snowy winter night, 38

So, What was My Bottom?, 31

South Africa, 17

SPCA (Society for the Prevention of Cruelty to Animals, 53

Speaking in his language, 72

spirit, 15, 148, 171

spiritual things, 15

Standing in the Peace of a Horse, 164

strong warrior

woman, 31

T

take time, 20
Tango, iv, 116, 117, 118, 119, 134, 135, 136, 137, 138, 139
Teaghlach: Celtic for Family, 122
That Sunday, 109
The barn swallows, 27
the choice, 31, 127
The Deepest Wounds Need the Deepest Healings, 140
the dreads, 99
The Horse Whisperer, 48
The Life Coaching Institute, 13
the Universe, 81
therapist, 34, 35, 40, 91, 113, 115, 116, 117, 118, 119, 121, 133, 157, 177, 180
therapists, 112, 120, 150
Tony Robbins, 13, 37, 177
trigger, 33
triumph, 99
Trudy, 44
trust, 73
Trust, 51
Trust!, 116
Tug of War, 133

U

Uncle Wilson, 173

V

very loving, 35

W

way of thinking, 43
Wayne Dyer, 13, 97
we got married, 39
We laugh, 37
whispering, or listening, 49
wild baboon, 18
wisdom, 8, 158, 170, 172

Y

You've Got to Have Friends, 78